# The American Utopian Adventure

TWELVE MONTHS IN NEW HARMONY

# TWELVE MONTHS

IN

# NEW-HARMONY;

PRESENTING A FAITHFUL ACCOUNT OF THE PRINCIPAL
OCCURRENCES WHICH HAVE TAKEN PLACE THERE
WITHIN THAT PERIOD; INTERSPERSED
WITH REMARKS.

## BY PAUL BROWN,

Author of 'A Disquisition on Faith;' 'Inquiry on Philosophic Education,' &c.

## PORCUPINE PRESS INC.
Philadelphia 1972

**Library of Congress Cataloging in Publication Data**

Brown, Paul.
    Twelve months in New Harmony.

    (The American utopian adventure)
    Reprint of the 1827 ed.
    1.  New Harmony, Ind.--History.  I.  Title.
F534.N5B8  1972        335'.9'77234            78-187438
ISBN 0-87991-000-3

First edition 1827 (Cincinnati: Printed and
Published by Wm. Hill Woodward, 1827)

Reprinted 1972 by Porcupine Press, Inc., 1317
Filbert St., Philadelphia, Pa. 19107, from a
copy in the collections of The Boston Public
Library

Manufactured in the United States of America

# TWELVE MONTHS

IN

# NEW-HARMONY.

For several years I had been addicted to the contemplation of a new social order, in which all property should be held in common stock, being fully persuaded that this was the only equitable mode of subsisting of mankind in a state of society. I was driven to meditate on this subject by my *suffering* from the inadequacy. of the existing institutions to extend justice to the poor, and the odious grinding influence of individual wealth and unequal usurped power, which in several instances. had borne grievously afflictively upon me. I became acquainted with several persons in New-York City and in the state of Ohio, who were in the same train of speculation. I saw a few passages of one Robert Owen's writing extracted into a pamphlet entitled "An Essay on Commonwealths," published by a Society in New-York. I afterwards saw a short letter from his hand, which had been published in a Limerick paper in reply to those who enquired of his sentiments concerning religion. I sought this Mr. Owen's works; but they were not to be found in print, in the country. There was some talk of this same Owen, who was represented as a man who was preaching the doctrine of the renovation of society in Scotland and Ireland, and who had even put his principles into operation at a place called New-Lanark in Scotland: As he was understood to be a man of ability and perseverance, it

was hoped that one day he might emigrate to this country, and make use of the plenty and cheapness of
vacant lands here, and the mildness of our general
government, to introduce into real life an example of
the sort of society that was so desirable to those who
speculated upon it, especially to those who suffered
from the abuses and degeneracy of the prevailing political authorities and institutions, whereby such as by mis-
fortune were destitute or unsuccessful, stood a very
inferior chance of a comfortable subsistence in the
general throng.  I thought much, and scribbled considerably on this subject; anticipated a multitude of
objections, which in my way I disposed of; and even
fancied I might in future afford a treatise that should
embrace the full theory and practice of this new and
strange model of society.  In the winter of 1824—25,
I was sojourning in Massachusetts.  I think it was in
the latter part of December, 1824, I received intelligence
by way of the papers, of the arrival of this same
Robert Owen at New-York, and his intended procedure
to the western states: whereupon I sat down and wrote
a letter to said Owen, to the following effect:

Sir—Being in a stage house in a neighboring village
a few days since, I laid my hands on the New-York
Statesman, which announced your arrival at that place
on your way to Harmonia.  I rejoiced at the prospect
which this degree of probability was able to bring to
light, of the recommendation of a theory which has been
a favorite speculation with me for a number of years.
More than seven years ago I gave a lecture on this
doctrine on Long Island.  The sentiments were gratifying to all free thinkers, but at that time had no practical effect.  Two years afterwards a commonwealth society was formed in New-York, whose scope
was to promote the establishment of commonwealths
or communities. I attended some of their meetings

In about a year a colony was here formed, that settled itself in Virginia. Two years ago I walked into the state of Kentucky on purpose to join myself with a society organized on your principles, but found no such. We have fallen upon a period when multitudes, shaking off the shackles of a superstitious and contracted education, make no difficulty in admitting that investigation is no crime. The age of reason has dawned. It is a crisis for the philanthropist to rejoice and to hope. With the multiplication of sects and parties of superstition, has increased the number of free thinkers. Even their Bible societies, their tract societies, and their reading societies, have ultimately some good effect, by giving numbers of ignorant vulgar a habit and relish of reading, whereby they acquire a curiosity which will not rest in Bibles, rituals, and the fantastical speculations of the priesthood.

Here is one argument which you had not in Britain, *i. e.* immense tracts of unoccupied soil are easily obtained in our western states. Even in Pennsylvania, which I deem more salubrious than the Ohio and Missisippi states, very large tracts are offered I think at two dollars fifty cents per acre on a long credit.—Inquired much for your works, but could find none—was edified by some extracts made by Dr. Blatchley. You will see for yourself the deficiencies in what attempts have been made towards establishments of commonwealths. Their permanence depends signally on education. They must be founded on the knowledge and clear conviction of the rights of human nature; but the principles can never be perpetuated and the establishment ensured from corruption, but by a critically modified system of education of youth. Indeed it is but extending the principle which is the well known source of all domestic happiness of social life, [I say *well known*, it being so at least to all studious moralists;] that is, a spirit of acquiescence and reciprocal yielding of the uses of things.

according to the exigencies of every one, without which no family is even at peace with itself.

The incomparable Mirabaud has a sentiment of this cast—"There exist, says he, no comforts in those families where the members are not in the happy disposition to lend each other mutual succours, to assist one another to support the sorrows of life, and to put away by united efforts those evils to which Nature has subjected them. The conjugal bonds are sweet only in proportion as they identify the interests of two beings united by the want of a legitimate pleasure, from whence results the maintenance of political society and the means of furnishing it with citizens. Friendship has charms only when it associates more particularly two virtuous beings, that is to say, animated with the sincere desire of conspiring to their reciprocal happiness." To build communities or commonwealths, is only to extend, habituate, and systematize, the application of this very principle. In fact, this modification of society is but a sort of regenerating of human character, and bringing to light that virtue and simplicity which have been long lost in the corruption and errors of ages, and left no advantages able to compensate them,—but of which yet the principle remains adherent to our constitution, and cannot be wholly extinguished whilst man is a social or gregarious being, or has any propensity to society.

To speak frankly, this piece of intelligence gave me more pleasure than did that of the landing of our justly honoured venerable Lafayette, which occasioned so much public rejoicing; and, as an omen, it may be more highly appreciated: for your visit, in the long and unseen concatenation of events, may be productive of consequences even more interesting to this nation and to the human race, than our first acquaintance with that illustrious genius.

The reason is, [be not offended,] I rejoiced at the prospect of those effects which the labours of one, who

I had grounds to believe, from what I had heard and read of your enterprizes on the other side of the water, possessed, from experience as well as talent, the skill and influence to bring into repute the doctrine of equality and unity of interest, to a degree superior to any whom I have observed to have made attempts in that way, would be likely to produce on certain portions of our population. If there is in the nature of things aught that I can do to propitiate or subserve your benevolent views, with the greatest pleasure I shall employ every opportunity of devoting my energy to that end. The cause of the renovation of society in a gradual and only way it can be brought about, whether in a small or large number, I consider as my own. All my studies are directed to this point. You will find a situation propitious for grounding of *scientific* communities, composed of such as living on the products of the soil (easily obtained) have abundant leisure for study and research.— Whatever I can do to facilitate your operations, in the service of this cause, I shall promptly attend. But, in point of these principles, I am an isolated individual, surrounded by a trading calculating multitude.

Accept the assurance of my esteem, and of my best wishes for your success.               P. BROWN.

Mr. Robert Owen.

This letter I directed to the Post Office of Harmony, which is in Indiana. Although the probability is that Robert Owen himself was at the City of Washington about the time when the mail containing my letter should reach Harmony, yet in his place one of his sons abode here; and there is no question that the letter ultimately came to hand according to its address. In the latter part of March, 1825, I sat out upon a journey into New-York state, and stopping in the neighborhood of Newburgh upon the North river, abode there seven or eight weeks, within which time, receiving two letters at once

by way of Poughkeepsie post-office from a man in Tennessee with whom I had corresponded, who herein making me very encouraging offers and more than confir-
matory of what he had before stipulated, I, writing him
a reply, was thenceforth under an obligation to make a
journey into Tennessee, which therefore I commenced
on the 13th of June. After reaching Albany by the river, I took the canal. I had much ado to make my way
through the country, for I was fain to make excursions
aside from the canal, to pick up some old out-standing
subscriptions for a book I had published, in order to be
able to defray my expenses. Moreover I had the advantage of the canal the greatest part of the way to Buffa-
loe: but stopping at Lockport I fell in with a Mr. Hawes, a
native or former resident of New-Braintree in Massachusetts, who reported that his son having been in the neighborhood of Harmony, stated as a fact that Robert Owen
had actually purchased of the Old German Harmonites
their town and whole estate: I could not fully credit this:
For I had not had the most distant surmise that he would
have completed a purchase and commenced a colony so
soon; for it was represented that the whole congrega-
tion of Rappites or old Harmonites had evacuated the
place, and numbers had settled under Owen. Hawes
had no doubt of it; and was anxious to go to the place,
saying he intended to embark as soon as he could take
his family with him. At parting he said these words—
"If you see Owen, tell him I intend to be with him, (at
Harmony) next winter. Tell him *my heart is there*, and
I intend to be there with my family next winter." From
Buffalo journeying on foot I reached Erie, where a young
man, having sojourned in Harmony, and having come
directly thence, confirmed the report of Hawes, and said
it was a fact that Owen had actually made the purchase,
and some hundreds of persons had congregated there
from various quarters. Pursuing my route to Pitt, I at
Meadville laid my hands on two Lectures of Mr. Owen,

delivered at Washington City in the preceding February and March. These I read with avidity. The owners made no difficulty of making me a present of them, setting but little value on them themselves. With these I was delighted for their novelty and the liberality of their sentiments. Here were many luminious sentences, and principles of the most philanthropic aspect. In all these I did not detect Owen's mercantile genius: but it must be allowed that he did not dwell much on absolute *common property.* Reaching the neighborhood of Pitt, I heard much talk of the promising state of Owen's new colony; that nine hundred persons were already collected there; that the numbers were increasing weekly, &c. At Pitt, Owen's lectures and plans were cash articles. A community was projecting there, and had its constitution in the press. But the gloss of the novelty of the thing was so ravishing, that the subject was generally never radically studied. I proceeded down to Cincinnati, and thence to Louisville. From this, with little difficulty I could have passed to New-Harmony, and had some encouragement so to do; but I had not been so contaminated by Owen's preaching of 'no merit nor demerit,' 'no praise nor blame,' (which indeed had not yet in full glare appeared in his writings) but that I had some sense of moral obligation, and on account of an agreement, felt myself obliged to go into the state of Tennessee, which therefore I did, by walking across Kentucky; and arrived in Overton County beyond the Cumberland river on the 26th of August, 1825.

Passing over the troubles of this journey of 1527 miles, in which I had suffered much, I found that Owen and his plans were the main talk even of Fisk the Collegian, the man with whom I dealt, who in all probability flattered himself inwardly with the persuasion (his knowledge of the world convincing him, no doubt, that there can scarce be a rich man but who is depraved and warped by wealth) that this said Owen was

2

very likely a brother *speculator in land, power, influence, riches, and the glories of this world*. Alas! as it fell out, his surmises were too well founded, and his opinion but too true; though perhaps the certainty of the thing the man never learned. Much appeared written in the National Intelligencer [a paper I frequently saw] on these topics, for and against Owen's doctrines. Having heard at Cincinnati that a paper was about to be es-tablished at New-Harmony, I wrote a letter to this latter place, of which the substance is what follows.

MR. OWEN THE YOUNGER.

SIR—I address this to you under the impression that your father is absent at Scotland, and for reasons, *at this time*, which you will observe below. I wrote to your father last winter, but gave my letter such a direc-tion, suspecting him to be on his journey to Harmony, that I have since found reasons for believing that it did not reach him at the time expected. At all events I had no reply. Have just arrived at this place by a route of more than 1500 miles, not having information till I had entered into engagements to come here and surmounted a part of my journey, that your father had made any purchase or commenced any establishment in this country. But a gentleman here, who was understood to be a free man, and well known to be opposed to slavery (both in principle and practice,) having desired me to come out and teach for him, I promised him my attendance; and having written again to him of the progress I had made, requesting a reply at a certain place, I felt myself under obligation to proceed, although I would rather have chosen to go to Harmony. I some-what disapprove a fashion prevailing in these southern regions, of putting children to Latin and Greek when eleven or twelve years old, and when altogether deficient in their vernacular language, which perhaps they are unable either to read or spell correctly. This is a prevailing rage among the quality throughout the southern states, [and even of some elderly studious people who have been accustomed when young to such an arrangement of studies] to spice their offspring with a smatter of the *dead languages*, even at the expense of an accurate knowledge of their own. At Meadville I met with your father's Lectures at Washington: I had previously seen a few passages of his writing elsewhere. There is a striking coincidence of his sentiments with my own. If I had the means I would with his leave republish his lectures and distribute them through the conntry. His new system of society has been a favorite speculation with me for many years.

One particular view I have in writing at the present time, is this. Having been informed that you had printing materials and were about establishing a paper at Harmony, I wish to know whether you have commenced printing a paper or not; and if you have, I wish you to send me two copies constantly, as often as published, as I wish to supply a friend at the northward. Have in time past published two books, of which I will endeavour to send you a copy of each. I am also willing, if you publish a paper for which so feeble a pen can adapt any thing, to furnish some communications, (perhaps in a scale of numbers,) if you will publish them; having, in two years past, written copiously what I thought I might revise at leisure in the latter part of my life, and sometime leave for the use of such as were prepared for it. But this subject of the remodelling the crasis of society, and perfecting our civilization, has been made an exceeding interesting one to the people of this country since the commencement of the current year; and it is not a time now to "place a candle under a bushel."

If I live, I expect to be a member of your society.

Please to give me a reply, at all events, giving information concerning your printing, and the circumstances of the community. The post office is kept at the very house where I live. The man who keeps it appears also favorably affected towards the new system of society; and probably may hereafter devote his whole interest to the cause.

With the most cordial wishes for your prosperity and the welfare of the community, I remain, sir, your constant friend,                           P. BROWN.

This letter I think I followed in three successive mails by two books and a pamphlet at an expense of postage nearly equal to their price, as presents to said Owen and their community. In the course of the winter I also sent forward packets of communications at several dollars' expense. I received no replies but the papers themselves, which came regularly to hand by the mail from the first numbers agreeably to my request. The liberal principles held forth in the prospectus of that paper (the New-Harmony Gazette) are well known to those among whom it circulated. In the first number appeared the constitution of the preliminary society, (preparatory to a perfect community) ratified the first of May, 1825. It appeared to be a very liberal one. Accompanying it was an address of Mr. Owen, in which he declared he wished to be considered on a level with the rest of the people, and a fellow member. The communications appeared to have been well received, for they were regularly inserted. It seems that one Jennings was at first for a while the Editor, and afterwards a Mr. Pelham, who continued so till near the close of the first year.— The last number I received before I left Tennessee, contained a new constitution, for a "New-Harmony community of equality," adopted on the 5th of February. This was the *perfect community* to which there had been allusion as what might be brought about in the course of three years. Mr. Owen had recently returned from his visit to Britain; and it seems that immediately on his arrival he professed the enthusiastic persuasion, that, contrary to all his former calculations, and with surprise, he found the people were at such a stage of progression as to be *then* fit to enter into a *perfect community!*

It may be proper in this place just to observe, that not a syllable was ever mentioned to me by Robert Owen or either of his sons, of any letters or any thing else having been received from me.

Now, then, having read Mr. Owen's writings very attentively through the course of about five months, and, from putting the most fair construction on them, inevitably drawing therefrom the conclusion that as a philanthropist he had for his single object to introduce a new system of society to gradually supersede the old, to exhibit an example to the world of a real commonwealth and a practicable process by which, at the present point of degeneracy in human morals and politics, reasoning men could in combinations throw themselves into the direct path to the perfection of our nature; it seeming to be as much a favorite object to him, as the discovery of perpetual motion has often been to an adventurer who has expended his whole fortune and a considerable part of his life in such a pursuit; and that no personal or family monopoly had any thing to do with his motives; I sat out in the month of March, 1826, upon a journey of 300 miles, to join him. At Nashville, by one who journeyed from New-Harmony, was put into my hands for the first time Owen's "New view of society, or essays on the formation of character." But it contained the identical doctrines set forth in the speeches and addresses published in his paper, which, in fact, were mostly harangues delivered some years before in London and Dublin. Arriving at Mount Vernon on the Indiana shore, I was astounded with the first intimation that negotiations for the security of the estate as private property with the interest of its value, were disturbing New-Harmony: that instead of a "community of equality," organized and fully settled under their new constitution, which I had read a few weeks before in the Gazette of the place; that constitution, which had appeared to be a very liberal one, was laid aside: and that the capital concern of the lord proprietor seemed to be to get an assemblage of people that were willing to sign a contract to pay for the estate at an appraisal that had been made, with the interest, within a certain time. I came into New-Harmony on the 2d day of April, 1826. It was any thing but a tranquil neighborhood. The impression I took from what I could gather, was, that this stipulation upon appraisal and with such conditions, not having been made to the people till they had signed the constitution, the disturbance first arose from some of them being backward and reluctant about taking such a yoke on themselves, which generally had not been expected; whereupon an advantage was immediately taken hereof by some aspiring aristocratical spirits, to make a division of the town into several societies, as one of the school, tavern, &c.; another of the mechanics, another [I think] of the farmers: the schooling and tavernkeeping principality offering to take on themselves the greatest part of the debt; exchanges to exist between these different bodies politic by what they called labor for labor. This was overruled by Mr. Owen, who refused to contract with them on such a plan, and declared he knew no parties in New-Harmony, and would countenance but one homogeneous union in that place. He afterwards shifted his ground, and said that in one society they could not exist, but there must be three.— In this he could not prevail. He next made a selection, and by a solemn examination constituted a nucleus of twenty-five men who answered in the affirmative to certain interrogatories; which nucleus were to admit members on the same grounds, the full members added having the same powers, Mr. Owen having a veto on every one to be admitted or rejected. One of the special engagements, one of the solemn affirmatives they were to make, was that they were willing to sign a contract with said Owen and William M'Clure, for the real and personal estate as appraised by somebody. All the full members as they were admitted, agreed to this.— There were three other grades of members—conditional members, probationary members, and persons upon trial. Another of the engagements was, to submit all the affairs of the community to the direction of Mr. Owen till two-thirds of them should think fit to govern themselves, provided the time be not less than twelve months. This it seems the people had sought, as there was not a concurrence to enforce the constitution.

When any man, who, having presented himself in the character of a philanthropist, and professed it his sole aim to substantiate an actual precedent of the true order of society, asks pay for his land or houses which he has destined for the foundation of such establishment, either principal or interest, to be secured as private property to himself or his heirs, from that moment he forfeits the confidence of all considerate persons who are in pursuit of realizing a true commonwealth upon earth. This was the beginning of Robert Owen's iniquities. The moment when this Mr. Robert Owen, after having made the public declarations, professions, and promises, which he had so widely done, having among other things proclaimed that the whole trading system was a system of deception, that property should be common, &c. made a motion to ask one single cent for the estate he had purchased professedly for the inheritence of a community, principal or interest, to be secured to him by the members who should inhabit it, as private property to himself or his heirs, he, by that very act, proved himself to have been insincere, proved himself to be a trading man and not a philanthropist, proved himself to be incapacitated in heart to found a real commonwealth, proved that it could not be the sole object and pursuit of his life to bring such a thing into existence, proved himself to be lacking of integrity, magnanimity, and all those solid sublime principles essentially requisite to form a character competent to introduce into life an example of a state of society in the true order of human perfection, and of a sort which he had recommended.⸳

Still we had hope—we that came hundreds of miles, impressed with the benevolence and energy of Mr. Owen's character, as an inference from his writings and in the full and fervent expectation of finding a commonwealth at New-Harmony, still had hope—hope of better things; we labored cheerfully, we endured inconveniences, we had patience to the last moment, we found every apology and justification for Mr. Owen as long as it was possible to find any. Alas! in the reality of things there was but too little ground for such hope, so long as such a man, clinging to individual wealth and practically justifying it, held the estate in his hands, and it rested at his will on what particular conditions it should be inherited, and of consequence what manner of persons should inherit it! Nevertheless, while it was inconvenient or scarce feasible to sojourn elsewhere, here were found some advantages in the place, particularly freedom of speech and of the press: for the press was *then* conducted in somewhat of accordance with the principles proclaimed in the prospectus: and was not restricted, and governed by favoritism and juntocraft.

Meetings were held every evening; and often several meetings in a day. The immigration to the place was great; and the nucleus often met to receive members, and to deliberate upon measures.

The task of managing all the affairs of the society no doubt was too complicate and burdensome for one mind, in the existing circumstances; and what must have made it tenfold more wearing, was the monstrous undertaking of keeping book accounts, and rounding the incomes and outgoes of the whole, every week, in dollars and cents. This very thing, also, was that which gave a disparaging and diminutive aspect to the project, as it tended to keep alive that suspicious and avaricious temper which is nourished by all the depraved institutions of the trading world. The keeping accounts of every pennyworth that was consumed, and of every hour's labour that was done, provided it chance to be *proved* or came under the eye of a reporter, setting them down as debt and credit, ranking persons in certain degrees of character according to the number of hours' work that appeared against their names on paper, was the sterile and tasteless drudgery of a number of intelligent persons, who otherwise might have been productive of the necessaries of life; but who herein were never free for any didactic or edifying intercourse, being bent, with their pens, over some sorts of legal or mercantile instruments. But these can never inspire a real community spirit: they intercept it. Depending upon these legal and mercantile tokens, estranges men from one another; it shews they have not a sufficient acquaintance to have confidence in each other: and the longer we accustom ourselves to depend on these things, the farther we are from that intimate acquaintance and mutual confidence. This depending on accounts, notes, bills, receipts, certificates, and reports on paper, for a knowledge of the relations in which they stand to each other, is a *proof*, and a *cause*, of men being strangers to each other's hearts. Mercantile ideas produce mercantile feelings—mercantile feelings produce distrust, suspicion, and avarice—distrust, suspicion, and avarice, produce litigious feelings—litigious feelings produce litigation, animosity, jangling, fighting, unequal division of property, and all the endless maze of mischiefs that the most corrupt stage of individual society is heir to. Hereby then we come back into the very plight from which we promised to enfranchise ourselves. So a system of merchandize, however ingeniously modified, does not seem to be the track by which to conduct people to a rational union of hearts and hands in the order of their perfection as intelligent and free as well as social beings.

Moreover, the dancing and the instrumental music engrossed more of the energy of speculation than the most important concerns. There must be a regular ball once a week, and a concert once a week.

There seemed to be a change of measures every week. There was not a vigilant perseverance in practice upon any one adopted process long enough to prove it effectually to be good or bad. Here were restless spirits continually urging some new experiment. It was proposed that the best of the buildings and land should be devoted exclusively to the use of the school; and the contract modified so that the community should take the poorest, but yet at too high a price. This was rejected by the nucleus altogether. Mr. Owen at that time explicitly approved of this rejection, and said he would have done the same thing. Mr. William M'Clure, it seemed, had a great estate, which, it had been represented, he had bequeathed expressly to promote communities (including a school) on the New-Harmony estate. It came out that he would not bestow any thing more than he had given, [this *giving* perhaps was to be *selling*, all the while] nor even leave a large and valuable Library and Museum which he had brought here for the express purpose, unless the school should be entirely separated from the rest of the society. Every republican was opposed to this division; and, among others, the principal teacher in the school establishment, strongly protested against it. The onset was revived in the course of two or three weeks, and the division being particularly urged by a female teacher, who is supposed to have had considerable influence with Owen, M'Clure, and others, (and who might possibly have some aspiring views to preroga-

tive and pre-eminence,) the importunity was so great
that it was even moved in a meeting of the nucleus, [Mr.
Owen *now* particularly recommending the measure] that
there be a resolution to submit to a meeting of the whole
population, whether they would be divided into four
distinct societies each signing its own contract, *i. e.* for
such a part of the property as it should purchase, each
managing its own affairs, [just as Mount Vernon, Vin-
cennes, or any other town] but to trade with one another by paper money. The resolution was carried. This
great meeting was held on the 28th of May, it being
Sunday. Two plans were proposed by Mr. Owen—the
first was, to have *one* community with different depart-
ments of occupations, having a set of officers to each,
as clerks, superintendents, &c. The other, to have
four separate societies. The first was not discussed at
all: The last, being more strongly recommended by Mr.
Owen, was immediately debated: but the meeting adjourned till evening, when, with a comparatively thin
assembly and some women being invited to vote while
others not knowing they should have a voice remaining
at home, besides many persons absenting themselves,
from a representation they had had in the meeting that
it was unlikely the thing would be decided that day, a
vote was thus hastily and unfairly obtained for this
strange division; which was afterwards said to be carried by a vast majority of the population! The doings
of this meeting knocked in the head all that had been
arranged or enacted by that of the first day of May, the
great anniversary of the founding of the society, when
Owen pompously preached of the mighty progress that
had been made in one twelvemonth from the commencement of the preliminary establishment, and admitted a
large number of persons, perhaps upwards of two hundred, probationary and conditional members, and persons on trial. Myself was of the probationers. Every
one had to sign some sort of paper. That of the proba-

tioners made mention of six months.  It bound them to accept as a full compensation for their services, their victuals and clothes, whether they should voluntarily withdraw, or whether they should not be received as full members.  All these things were turned up side down by this last meeting, four weeks afterwards.  All distinctions of members being levelled for the purpose of voting in this assembly, every person was obliged to make application anew to some one of these particular societies, according to its peculiar regulations, or be no member of any society at all.  Many withdrew disgusted, and left the town; many lingered till it should be convenient to remove; and would enter into no engagements.  Now, new contracts must be made out for all these separate parcels of property: Wm. M'Clure was to pay down into Mr. Owen's hands a certain number of thousands of dollars, in part pay for the school society's purchase.

Thus all the lingering turmoils of this place, all the agitations, all the embarrassments that have prevented a peaceful union of these people, appear to have originated from a solicitude about *private exclusive property.* This is what the people left the old establishments to get rid of; this is what they came here to respire from; and they but rushed into the very vortex of its effervescence.  Mr. Owen was very anxious to secure by contract the value of the land, with profits on what he had paid, and the interest; the whole to be paid in certain instalments, and all within a certain time; if not so paid, to have the estate revert to the original owners or their heirs.  Mr. M'Clure was very solicitous that the private property *he* should bestow (or loan) should be appropriated in such a particular way, according to his own peculiar favorite views, and no other way forever; and to ensure contrivances that should raise profits thereon to keep the fund good and upon the increase.  Numbers of worldly-minded persons here, who were at heart opposed to the social system, and would choose rather to bring things back exactly to the exclusive system as in other populous towns, it is supposed seized the opportunity to use their influence with M'Clure and the rest of the population, to counteract the expansion of republican principles. And this overweening care and anxiety about *individual exclusive property*, (which it is the very essence of a community to subvert) has given rise to all the troubles of this place.

When an individual bequeaths a valuable legacy to a college or any other particular institution, or to be retained as a fund, the interest to be appropriated in a particular way that is designated, the laws make it always so appropriable, and it can never be otherwise appropriated if there remain any persons to advert to it. No other appropriation could hold it if the law be put into effect.

The instituting of such amusements as public balls, promenades, and music, seemed to be propitious to interest the young, and enamour them of the place. But the constant succession of this sort of things, clearly induced volatility, and aversion to serious duties.

The boys were to be retained in school till the age of 18. From 16 to 18 they were to learn trades. They were to be managed so that each might learn a part of a trade, and be all the while sensible of their dependence on each other in their work. Young *can* be brought up in such circumstances, by properly enlightening their minds, as to be a fraternity of free men, having correct and enlarged views of human nature, and a cordial spirit of co-operative union;—and they *can* be trained so as to be obsequious machines operating unitedly to the views of a sovereign lord proprietor who supervises and controls them and takes the profits of their products, and who prevails to engross their affection and veneration, so that they feel interested in such coincidence of their efforts, till he can even manage them as he pleases. This were a sort of union and fraternity of subjects of a despot. It were a community of *canaille* kept under the control of aristocracy. It would not bear much light:—Expansion of mind among the people would break its main spring. If men can be moulded into what character one pleases, by *circumstances* skilfully managed, it is not worthy of a philanthropist to make them take the character of cupidity of wealth, nor of implicit devotion to an individual. They should follow the oracles of nature.

It has been said that Mr. Owen gave but $128,000 for the whole estate, including about 28,000 acres of land, the village of Harmony, and some stock, goods, and furniture. He sold off two lots to separate communities, for about $12,000, with interest at 5 per cent. from the date of sale; the pay day of the principal to be at twelve years. The village of Harmony, with some personal property or moveable goods and 25,00 acres of land, it seems, was appraised at $140,000. The agreement with all the full members was, that they should sign a contract to pay for it at the valuation. It seems, by all account, that $20,000 more were demanded by Owen to be added to it, to make up what in *his* judgment the valuation *would* have been· by the same persons on a credit of twelve years; and that thence the sum in the written contract was to be in reality $160,000 principal, to be on interest at 5 per cent. from date, to be paid annually and the principal to be paid in instalments, one of which [I think of $50,000] in three years from date, another in seven years, and so on, till the payment should be completed at twelve years. But this $20,000, [the people protesting against it] was rescinded, and the contract remained $140,000. If the fulfilment finally failed for one year after the last due, the estate to revert to Owen and M'Clure or their heirs, who were never to appropriate it to any other purpose but the inheritance of communities. But what other tribunal but *their judgment* should decide the nature of these communities? and what do such individuals now call communities? and how well do they agree among themselves about the definition of community? The remainder of the land, of this whole Harmony estate, which is about four fifths of it or more, is worth surely as much as the other part. So that for one half of the value of the property, [including no more than a fifth of the land] Mr. Owen was getting at least upwards of $20,000 more than he gave for the *whole*, and insurance of annual interest on the whole money! This is the man who, while he preached, spake of 'common property,' 'perfect equality,' 'perfect communities,' 'the pernicious and fatal tendency of *individual property*,' and the villainous nature of trade.—When the Fox preaches, let the Geese beware.

Some of the nucleus objected to the contract on account of the *reversion*. But before this contract had a chance to be executed, [though he professed he was ready, but that he only waited for the attendance of his lawyer to transcribe and finish the instrument] Mr. Owen strongly recommended the division.—By that division, this embryo-bargain was knocked in the head, and new ones grew up. Moreover, after the division was put beyond question and some arrangements commenced, Mr. Owen is said to have brought in *another* charge, asking or urging the people to bind themselves to pay, on account of the bankruptcy of the old preliminary society. For there had been some sinking of Mr. Owen's funds in his absence, by the preliminary society, of some twenty or thirty thousand dollars. Now, those who made the debt were gone. It was proposed that the generation who remained here and should buy the land, should pay the debt: as it is written, " the fathers have eaten of the sour grapes, and the children's teeth are set on edge," &c.

This plan of a division of the town and responsibility

for the property, disgusted the most sincere and considerate advocates of the social system in the place. It appeared an intricate refined system of merchandize. For there was to be a society of external commerce, of manufactures and trades, of agriculture, and of education and literature,—and a general merchant-magazine to receive all the surplus from each, to go to pay the debts, as it should be turned into money: that of external commerce only should trade with the world; in other respects the societies should only trade with one another by *labor notes*. Each 'should get labor notes for the products it put into the magazine *when they should be disposed of*. They were under a necessity of trade, and with a circumscription where and with whom they should trade. They must trade or die, and they *must* trade with just such societies and at such places, and no other. Several withdrew; and many began to look to some other quarter for realizing the existence of the principle that had been professed, detecting fresh proofs of the hollowness of the ground upon which they had been building their hopes. Directly after the division, the commercial society seems to have been abolished, or reduced to the agency of Mr. Owen, he proposing to keep the store and tavern till such time as he could, by their profits of trade, retrieve the value of the preliminary debt: thus he appears willing to shift into the characters of a retailer and tavern keeper, to save by ninepenny and four-pence-half-penny gains, after the manner of pedlars, the money which he had lost, probably 30,000 dollars, to keep the community fund good; although in his preaching he had avowed his conviction that as soon as by a fair specimen their overwhelming advantages should be elicited, it would be impossible to provide these *new arrangements* so fast as the people of general society would want them; thus admitting implicitly, as a consequence, that as they would build for themselves and rush spontaneously into an imitation of what had.

such conspicuous eligibility, ONE PROTOTYPE of a real republican community, displayed to the world, a living proof of its peculiar advantages and distinguishing dignity as an improvement of human character, would do more execution towards the spread of the principle than millions of money without it.

The mechanics and manufacturers had, without a dissenting voice, united themselves into one society. Then this and the farmers' negotiated about uniting and forming one; but did not. To keep up the stream of bargaining and altering of bargains, it seems there was some shifting of the arrangements about the store and tavern; that afterwards the tavern was sold or hired to the farming society, and the store divided, Owen taking one part of it, and I think the mechanics' society the other, and perhaps rendering to Owen statedly a part of the profits.

Mr. Owen seems to have constantly inculcated upon these people from the beginning, lessons of thrift, and knacks of saving and gaining money. Yet persons were spending their time in teaching music and dancing; profusion of musical instruments were provided, and great quantities of candles burnt at their balls. It is said he once told them in his preaching, that they 'must be *great misers.*' A great part of the time the people were very much stinted in their allowances of coffee and tea, butter, milk, &c. Mr. Owen, constantly boarding at the tavern where luxurious regale was copiously provided to sell to travelling men of the world and loungers, for money, drank rich coffee and tea; while the multitude of laboring people who quartered in the large boarding houses, being circumscribed in their rations, were very much in the habit of drinking rye coffee, or rye mixed with store coffee.—The gardens were awfully neglected; though several professed gardeners were in the society. Much ground lay fallow that might have made handsome gardens. The people instead of employing their thoughts to execute their work well, were musing on plans of new arrangements and changes of measures in the system of the government of the society, the purchase, the contracts, &c. &c. The system of reporting by hours' labour, and keeping debt and credit, was a leaden weight upon some that would work from *principle.* I labored attentively in taking care of several gardens, to add to the general stock of vegetable productions—but had no credit given me (as I suppose) in the general reporting office for three-fifths of what I did; not being seen by the proper persons to put down my name on paper, and it being against my principles to keep debt or credit in a community. The mischief was, that some of these gardens were called *private* gardens. Of this piece of ground supposed to be occupied by a community, of common property, some was called *private ground* and some *public ground!* those who labored on the private ground, were not considered as laboring for the community. The dressing of the vegetables was done extreme slightly by some of the gardeners and the boys under them. So that there was always a scarcity of garden vegetables. There were times when no more than three pints of milk were allowed a day for six persons, and one half pound of coffee and two ounces of tea per week. Every thing was at six and seven. The place was full of clamour, disaffection, and calumny. Even salads were deposited in the store, to be handed out—making ten thousand unnecessary steps, and causing them to come to the tables in a wilted deadened state. It often happened that some houses got a greater share of provisions than others.

It has been recollected by some discreet and observing persons who had been constantly on the estate from the purchase and settlement, that Mr. Owen, in an address to the people immediately previous to his departure for Scotland in the summer of 1825, said to them, that on his return he would divide his fortune with them; saying, "when I return I will set every thing right; and will divide my fortune with you." The mass of the people here were of so light, equivocal, and desultory a cast of mind, that scarce one was to be found who had a trace on his memory of this important part of that address. But several persons in the new communities, Nos. 2 and 3, distinctly recollected it; and are positive that he seriously made that statement. It is also recollected that he said he *would take all the loss on himself.*

The school society made a contract for 900 acres of land and the best of the buildings for about $49,000 on interest of 5 per cent, which they borrowed of M'Clure, and took a lease for 10,000 years, to pay him the interest, the lease being assigned to him by Owen, the principal to be paid after seven years in equal instalments. This society I think took on itself the title of the 'New-Harmony community of equality of rights and duties, and common property.'

Mr. Ludlow handed Mr. Owen a very plain letter on Saturday. He read it (though against himself) to the meeting on Sunday, the 18th [June.] He made some reply in words, which Ludlow, not being present to hear, writes an answer to; and prepares to take his departure for the North.

Now, to carry on the farce, legal and formal contracts must be made with all these societies, conveying the parcels of property attached to them. The mechanics entered into indenture with Owen for land and houses for about 23,000 dollars, to be paid in instalments after five years, to the end of twelve, with interest of 5 per cent from the beginning; he giving but a lease instead of a deed, to be given up for a deed when the instalments are paid; but if not paid, this whole estate is to revert to the originals, heirs or assigns: so that this lease, though of long term, is but a beguiling sound for any other purpose than to secure the possession for the present till a trial be made to pay the instalments, as soon as one of which fails, the lease is void.—This indenture was printed in sufficient numbers to supply every member, and some others. There was to be another indenture to convey the personal property, as the tools, goods, stock, &c. which was to be at about 20,000 dollars: this I suppose was printed. The like was to be done with the farmers' or pastoral society: which undoubtedly were finished; for some few families signed contracts and remained drudging on the farm, though many scattered away. So here were four long, solemn, solid contracts or indentures, of several octavo pages, built up, as strong as fire and water could make them, to convey the real and personal property to these two societies and secure the pay and interest for it.

Something of mystery hung over the real motives of this strange division of the town; and people had various conjectures about them. Some of the most ingenuous and considerate, who felt no interest in any particular party and had no more acquaintance with one than another, had such thoughts as these, viz. that there was a great want of ingenuousness, liberality, and every thing like a community spirit, discoverable at the root of this separation of the school society from others, seeing it clearly carried the marks of an aristocratical and exclusive spirit, inasmuch as the few projectors of it being extremely wealthy, they could thereby have opportunity to make a common stock which should circumscribe the participation of their wealth to a few favorites. This were sporting with the feelings of a multitude of poor, but honest, industrious farmers and mechanics, who were equally susceptible of being led by plain reasoning and kind treatment and good examples, into a habitual cultivation of all the true principles of a well organized commonwealth.—Does this savour of that benevolent disposition which is the harbinger of the amelioration of human society? Is this what characterizes the philanthropist, who sincerely aims at promoting union, and to extend the blessings of peace, plenty, and the reformation of morals, among his fellow beings? What matters it whether it is *one* man or a *few* men that shall exclude their superfluous wealth from the participation of all others? It is aristocracy, it is oppression, it is want of sympathy, it is want of benevolence, it is want of justice! These few had wealth, a vast superfluity of possessions more than by the law of nature they had any right to: they would not share it with the people of New-Harmony; they would exclude the majority of them;—they would not make common stock with the multitude or as many as would acquiesce in the principle and coincide with them in this particular, to such a number as could subsist in the place:—no—they would circumscribe this wealth to themselves and a few favorites which they should select or admit; a small choice company should enjoy the benefits of this wealth, such as twenty or thirty [besides the scholars,] and all others be excluded. These few, because some of them by chance had a redundance of individual wealth, must have a permanent situation, secure from embarrassment; while the others, because they mostly happened to be poor, must *remain* poor, or be slaves or vagrants. What is this but aristocracy? They partition the wealth of New-Harmony; the greatest part of it they determine to keep in a small compass; they say, 'he that hath, to him shall be given, that he may have more abundance—but from him that hath not, shall be taken away even that which he seemeth to have.' All that came to New-Harmony to compose a community, came to convert their private property to *common* property. There is no other way to form a community. If those who have most, separate it and exclude all the rest, they certainly came not here with such a spirit, for they prove that they do not measure men's rights by the law of nature, but by the maxims of the exclusive system under the aristocratical institutions of the world; and acknowledge that they that *have* most, have a *right* to most. Does this argue that expansive, magnanimous philanthropy, characteristic of the benefactors and reformers of mankind? Or does it announce a partial, selfish, contracted, sullen, suspicious spirit? Moreover, many were leaving one society and joining another; and numbers flocked into the school society; so that they had a multitude of different sorts of mechanics, as well as farmers and gardeners.—Reader, please to bear in mind that it is a FARCE of which we are recounting the events, and recollect that in a play the scene changes oftener than in real life. In a little time those few that were individually rich, one after another had scattered themselves away to the four winds—and had they remained they had made no common stock; for an article of their constitution bound every member to put all his available property (thro' the hands of the treasurer) into some bank of the United States; neither he nor the society to have right to make use of principal or interest, till he should leave the society, when he should have his money with its interest, as private property. So that there never has been any sample of such a thing as a real, general common stock, brought into being in this place: and Mr. Owen's example and practical schemes have directly opposed it.

Some thought Mr. Owen's avarice was the root of the division—(indeed it rested on his will, and without his sanctioning the measure it could never have gone into effect;) for he had above 30,000 dollars paid down to him by M'Clure, and whether he was to have greater pay for his property by this retailing way or not, he might think he could get more satisfactory security for it on these smaller sums from separate societies. But let us take a fair look at the immediate effects of this division.—Many were disappointed, and unavoidably chagrined, at such tergiversation, whiffling, and unnecessary overturning of things: they were completely nonplussed, justly conceiving themselves wronged and ill treated, after having journeyed scores or hundreds of miles with the expectation of finding a community; their hopes having been inspired by statements that issued from this place or from the pen of Mr. Owen; and among these some of the most industrious and faithful and such as from principle willingly did their part in the general labor. The opening of such sure sources of jealousy and contention, did not fail to dishearten them: and such proofs of partiality and pharisaical ambition, as well as an overweening solicitude for private wealth, was effectual to disgust them and to shake their confidence in those who had pledged themselves to assist them and lead them into the right way. Those really fit to enter into a republican union, were disgusted at being approached nearer to the state of individual property than before. The farmers were spiritless and discouraged; for the best of their land and orcharding was wrested from them and partitioned to the other societies; and the moment the best garden in town began to abound with fruit, it was assigned to the *mechanics*, and taken from those who had labored in it. The claim of some crops being unsettled between two societies, a large patch of cabbages went to ruin by weeds; and every thing was at six and seven, at the very time when every thing ought to have been in complete order and people attending busily to saving the products.

June 25th, Sunday evening, Mr. Owen harangued the people, addressing their passions,—told them how to be *successful*. What is this *success* he speaks of? Not living tranquil and happy; but [more likely] *getting rich* so as to pay him his money and make sure of their land. That seemed to have been the evident view, to make such impression, without regard to enlarging their knowledge so as to comprehend *his* motives. Moreover, these gradually come to light. The eyes of many are opened It cannot be denied that he is anxious to save his money. It is abundantly manifest that he belies his former· professions and promises. Many have of late moved away [July 17,] several of the farmers, and some of the mechanics, and even some of the school society. Some of the members of the different societies changed their places and joined others. A spirit of tergiversation was infused, was encouraged, and began to operate powerfully, even among those who were otherwise the most seriously disposed and inclined to constancy by the circumstances of their education and habitual carriage. At last it seemed eligible to some to recur to their former resources in general society, though betided with many gloomy recollections; rather than to plunge into slavery and certain dependence by incurring a debt that had ten chances to one, not to be paid, and where was almost a certainty of some failure on the stipulations of the contract, to make the estate revert to its original owners, or heirs; which there was manifestly no way to prevent but slavish labor and privation, or else slavish trading. Any thing better than this, must have depended in the first instance upon many individuals among the members having rich private fortunes, which was not known to Mr. Owen nor to every one of the members;—and, in the second place, upon their rendering up and devoting those estates, to liquidate the common debt, and promote the general good; of which was no institute. Even Mr. Owen had not, from the beginning, made it a condition of admittance to membership, that each should convert what he had to common stock. Therefore no such thing was calculated. In the school society indeed, they agreed to give their loose effects, such as money, to the treasurer, to be put into some bank, so that they could not live individually upon their private estates, but to lie at interest, which each should draw with his principle whenever he should leave; and he might leave any day. So these rich individuals were to run no risk; their private fortunes were to be secure at all events; and it was not necessary for them to be sincere votaries of the cause which they were associated under pretence of following: for they did not contemn and suppress the respect of wealth; they took measures to nourish it; they were sure they could take more liberties than the poor, since they were conscious that all would look to them as the stay of the institution, wherefore they could give themselves leisure without even incurring the reproaches of others or the danger of exciting ill feelings; while those who had nothing, must labor and devote their time, not knowing but elsewhere they might have earned a competence with less anxiety in the same time; whereas here in three years they might be as destitute as ever: indeed in two years, for it would be much if they could pay their interest within a year's indulgence. But in the other societies, persons could hold private wealth in their pockets, in their chests, or at a distance in stock, houses and lands.

The people of this town continued strangers to each other in spite of all their meetings, their balls, their concerts, and their so frequent occasions of congregating in the Hall, and all their pretence of co-operation. From the time I first set my feet within this little town of about one half mile square, I think there is not within the range of my observations during my former travels, any other town in the United States where the same number of persons living together within such a compass, for so many weeks and months, and daily and hourly passing and repassing each other, were so perfectly strangers, and void of all personal intimacy with each other's feelings, views, situations, and [very generally] names.

On the 4th of July Mr. Owen delivered his declaration of mental independence, to an assembly in the Hall. It was a very rainy day. He pointed out religion or superstition, individual exclusive property, and politi-

5

cal or legal marriage founded on one or both of the former, as the tripleheaded cause of the moral evil and misery of the earth. He has spoken much of this being the first time these truths were promulgated to the world. Now, different persons had written upon these subjects severally, long ago. One or more authors had picked the whole fabric of theology to pieces many years before he was born; and the Godwins, the Woolstoncrafts, and others, before his time, had written against individual property, and against marriage. All the originality that pertained to Mr. Owen in this thing, consisted in these two circumstances:—1st. His uniting or assembling together these three causes into one, as being jointly concerned in the production of evil; and 2d. His proclaiming the doctrine *orally* to an assembly of people:—Whereas others had only written, in books, separately on each of these subjects: and some of their works were posthumously published. For this much originality and use, he ought to have credit.

I joined myself to the English farmers, or what was called Community No. 3, and abode with them a short time: then retired a few miles in the country where I abode three or four weeks, still regularly visiting Harmony very frequently, noting all that of importance occurred.

About this time Owen was delivering an excellent course of lectures on early education; which was done at the Hall on Sunday evenings. At the close of one of which [perhaps the last] his son, Robert Dale Owen, who was then superintendent general of the education society, stood up, and addressing the people, made demand of certain stipulated [or understood] pay to be advanced for the tuition of the other societies' children; alleging it was impossible without it for them to exist as a society.

The education society appeared at that time to be very industriously preparing substantial and pleasant accommodations for a permanent community.

I returned, [August 8th] and sojourning a week or two with the pastorals or farmers, next associated with the mechanics, whom I assisted in their out-door labor, attendance upon the sick, &c. Every thing was at loose ends, and though many applications were made, they demurred acting on them, and received no members. I assisted a number of days at harvesting their apples, which, though not perfectly ripe, were so exposed to the depredations of the "children of this world," that it was thought economical to gather them. They were tumbled into a close room in a new unfinished brick building, in open hogsheads and on the floor, and instead of being distributed to the people at once, lay there till the greatest part of them went to ruin. The indentures, one or both, remained unexecuted, and even if they had been executed, a clause in the agreements gave Mr. Owen a *veto* upon every member: in other words, he was to have a right to object to and keep out whom he pleased. So that these things being undecided, there were in fact no real members to the society, but only they hung together by the sufferance of Mr. Owen, who was still lord proprietor of the houses and lands, inasmuch as the contracts were not completely executed; [and perhaps not intended to be—other things were brewing;] much less could they take in any new members. Meanwhile a diversity of offices remaining in this society, as of superintendent, intendents, &c., which occasioned perplexity and hindrance, the people held a meeting, in which they came to the bold and extraordinary resolution to abolish all offices then existing, and appointed three men as DICTATORS and sole directors of all the movements and arrangements in the society. These three persons were called the TRINITY; the oldest or first person being called God the Father, the second God the Son, and the third the Holy Ghost. But their reign was short; as we shall see by and by.

To return to the school affairs.—The farmers or pastorals determined to withdraw their children from the boarding school, but were willing to pay for the tuition they had received. The mechanics refused to pay at all, and thenceforth their children were considered as withdrawn, and their attendance stopped. The gardens and fields were almost entirely neglected. The weeds grew as high as the houses. Large holes made by brutes and boys in the decayed fences of the enclosures, still grew wider (instead of smaller), and swine ranged at pleasure throughout—next cows—next horses; and whole lots of cabbages, beans, potatoes, pumpkins, and cucumbers, became common stock to the community of hogs, neat cattle, horses, and poultry. These, marking no particular grades of rank, were all "full members." [I ask pardon for saying in another place that there had been no specimen of common stock in this town, forgetting that of these sorts of innocent animals, which is the *only* specimen; and this people, though of different species, lived very amicably together.]—The people were at swords' points in the two parts of the town, about the school and other things: no town outvied it in party feelings. A pilfering disposition very much prevailed; and scarce a week passed but shirts, handkerchiefs, or stockings, were filched from some persons out of the laundries or yards of the boarding houses. A battle was fought with fists, about the last of September, between two dames of the house called 'number 4,' where abode the farmers and shepherds. I do not exactly know the cause, but think it was something about theft or laziness. The children ran mad, in point of morals, from having heard the doctrine of no 'praise nor blame, no reward nor punishment,' which went under the name of the NEW SYSTEM. Coercive discipline was called the OLD SYSTEM.

After his course of lectures on education, Mr. Owen had proposed to the people a 'community education,' wherein the children should meet him at the Hall three evenings in a week, conducted by their ushers or tutors, and accompanied by their parents and others, and be taught and examined in public. This was heralded as a measure of incalculable utility. It was said that in an incredibly short time, by this community education, the children would have made such surprising progression in the accumulation of knowledge, as to be able to teach their parents; and the people of the place generally would be so thoroughly changed in their minds and hearts, as to be fit members of a community! Its acceptance was carried by vote.

The farmers and mechanics conferred on a combination to educate their children together at one school:—they agreed upon it. Here were, I think, near two hundred children to be taught. Mr. Owen was the confest leader and director in this great concern; he having influence, and property, and command, and the mass of the people thinking there was no one that knew so much as he. He expressly preferred young, inexperienced men, who had never taught in any school at all, as being more susceptible of his particular theory and practice: and this he recommended to the people in assembly, when they would have otherwise taken in persons for that purpose, who were experienced, and advanced in life.

A number of papers from me rested on the printer's file, as accepted and approved by the editor. Mr. Owen became the editor and conductor of the paper himself; the other man being discharged or resigning: indeed he never was treated well in his office, being often interfered with or slighted. Even those papers which came by mail from Tennessee, were not all published. After a suspension of four or five weeks, [recommended by the former editor] the printer having put the next in type, Mr. Owen [according to the statement of this printer] explicitly forbade him to publish any more of those papers, and said he was sorry he had inserted this. I had heard several persons speak favorably of these papers, but none speak against them. I speak of such as had appeared in the Gazette. They were all of the same principles, and similar style. Mr. Owen himself had spoken well of them publicly to the people, recommending their perusal. Moreover the printer represented that some young persons had spoken against them as become irksome, but could not tell who. Under these considerations I wrote a letter to Owen, as follows:

*Mr. Robert Owen, Editor of the New-Harmony Gazette.*

NEW-HARMONY, AUG. 28, 1826.

SIR—

As thirty-four numbers of a series of communications had been handed forward for publication in the Gazette, thirty-one of which had gone into the printer's hands, and were accepted and approved by the preceding editors in so far as to publish twenty-eight; at the conjuncture of publishing which last, the printer stated he had received express orders from you to publish no more—saying you were sorry he inserted *that*, that they had become "so objectionable" that they must be discontinued; intimating that they were worn out, &c.—observing, besides, that he had given you the three succeeding numbers and you had returned them with the above interdiction, wherefore it was supposed you had inspected them; I take the liberty to inquire of you wherein those three next numbers, twenty-nine, thirty, and thirty-one were so objectionable, or what there might be in particular in the six numbers (which were prepared) up to thirty-four, that made them unworthy of a place in that paper, more than the others. As all I had heard concerning them from persons abroad, was favorable to the others, and not finding any instance of a person speaking otherwise of them *here*, except the printer, this seemed worthy of inquiry. Please to give me an answer in writing, pointing out the faults in those three numbers. Yours, with much consideration,

P. BROWN.

About the same time I also sent him a short, plain scheme of education, calculated and proposed for the practice of a community, taking children from birth, and extending to the highest branches of the sciences, asking him to publish it in his Gazette. After the lapse of a few days, this paper, together with the letter, were returned to me through the hands of the former editor, by whom they had been sent forward, without a word being said why he did not publish it, or on what account he objected to any thing of my writing, except that he made declaration that, with reference to the papers the letter spoke of, *he had not read them.* Now he undoubtedly forbade the printer to publish any more of them, and expressed his regret that the printer had set in type the last then in print. And this is a rather odd and curious fashion, for an editor to condemn and reject, without reading, what had been received, and the former editors had approved; especially when himself had commended the tenor of the series of which this was a part, and of the same style and principles. However, the printer said he had given the papers into Owen's hands, who afterwards returned them, and, as if he had inspected them, forbade their publication, saying they had 'become so objectionable' that they must be discontinued. Hereafter we have his own declaration that *he had not read them.* So that here is confessedly a prohibition to publish, and regret that any part was *then* printed, of course a rejection, of things without examination, without reading. Does this agree with the stipulations in the prospectus of the New-Harmony Gazette? As the papers had been delivered back into my hands, it was advised by this man who had been the editor for near a year past, a man of reflection and talents, and a sound judgment, to hand Owen the communications that remained, that he might read them, and know what they contained; which appeared to me eligible, that he should at least be presented with the two which had lain on hand so long and had been sent such a distance at expense; as it seemed altogether proper that an editor should see and examine the things he rejected, especially when they had been approved by his predecessors. Whereupon it was agreed that the whole of those papers should be handed to Owen for his particular examination; which afterwards was accordingly done. Nothing came to my ear concerning them; but after a few days, one or two of them, the next in the order of the series to those which had been printed, were delivered to the printer for publication; one of which soon appeared; and the other a few weeks afterwards.

Mr. Owen went about setting up his school. The chambers of the shoe factory were prepared, for its accommodation. He brought some large maps into the Hall, on which the children were to be exercised: and, usually bringing in globes in the evening, the education went on according to appointment. The children were made to point out the names and situations of places on these maps and globes, and to answer a few questions concerning the motions, shape, and size of the world, &c, the effect of all which was said to infuse real general knowledge; which indeed seemed to be nothing but some degree of *faith:* for they received only upon Mr. Owen's authority that such were the names of such places, and that they had such situations as were represented by certain marks, figures, and shades, upon the map, which verily were but faint and fallacious images of the reality of the appearance of places that were 10,000 miles distant, which the children never saw, and were never likely to see; and which Owen himself never having seen nor touched, had no *knowledge* of their particular existence, but only *faith*. Owen and his young teachers exercised them in a similar way at the shoe factory, and once a day took them in procession to the Hall, besides three nights in a week, and once every Sunday. This teaching went on perhaps six weeks. Now, the Hall was the property of the education society, having been purchased with the other buildings, and valued at $9,000. This was included with the church or work-shop, the granaries, the boarding school, 'Number five,' or mansion house of Father Rapp, 'Number four,' and many other dwelling houses, and chiefly paid for, as I observed before. To return: within the few remaining days of my sojourn with the mechanics, I prepared to give the people a discourse on the grounds and indications of mutual confidence, with reference to commonwealths. Several lectures I had offered, particularly two delivered in April and May, which I aimed at adapting to the circumstances of the crisis, had but thin audiences; the people being fatigued with meetings, chose rather to walk, and take their recreations on Sundays. Mr. Owen constantly using the Hall at ten or eleven o'clock every Sunday morning, for his school, I asked him early in the week, if the Hall was to be occupied for any purpose about eight or nine o'clock the next Sunday morning, or whether it would be admissible to deliver a lecture there at that time: and he gave me to understand that any time between eight and ten the place would be accessible for such purpose. Hereupon I gave written notice at three public places three or four days previous, of my intention to lecture on an important subject at such a time: not, however, mentioning the particular topics upon which I should discourse: therefore, on Sunday, the 10th day of September, a number of people being together in the Hall about the time specified, I discoursed to them as follows:—

The only way to establish a community in the next

6

generation, [or rather to ensure such establishment to take place] is supposed to be to train the children of the present generation in a uniform systematic mode calculated to imbue them with liberal sentiments, congenial feelings, and the principles of union and common property, whereby these children's *children* being likewise brought up by persons possessing such principles and making an experiment of living in a conformity with them, will naturally come into the order, and without difficulty remain in a state of harmony and cooperation, and think of individual detached interests but with the utmost contempt. This is sure, and in the highest degree laudable, and important.

But there is another desideratum which engages the feelings of some contemplative and considerate philanthropists, which by no means precludes this which I have just mentioned; and that is, to form a community or republican commonwealth among those grown people of the present existing generation, who are true converts to the doctrine of the renovation, who are fully convinced of the sources of moral evil and all the miseries infesting human society, who have renounced the old institutions of the world, who are willing to return into the order of human perfection, and who are prepared to enter immediately into the practical application of their principles. *These*, too, are desirous to form a community, of themselves. These grown persons, middle-aged persons, and elderly persons, who having long and maturely ruminated on this subject, are firmly and conscientiously determined to renounce every individual pre-eminence for the superior advantages of this mode of subsistence, are solicitous to realize the happiness of passing the remainder of their days in a condition of equality of enjoyments, common interest, common possession, and reciprocal complacency. They arrive at this plight of soul by similar trains of reasoning. They have the same mode of arguing: and they come to the conclusion that there is no other foundation for perfect equity. They have experienced troubles which they have been obliged to ascribe to the existing institutions. These have forced them to reflect. They have come to a full view of the simple universal rights of human beings; they have a glimpse of the chain of causes that infallibly leads to their perfection; they see the degeneracy of fashionable politics; they see the corrupt deceitfulness of the present constitution of society; they sigh for an opportunity to introduce and to substantiate beyond the possibility of defeat, a new and a better structure more propitious to the security of our greatest good; even a new system of social life, more congenial to truth and to nature.

But it is said [and justly] we must first have confidence in those with whom we connect ourselves by community of property. Very little reflection will make us see that it is but for these people to know one another, to make them have confidence in each other—that is, to be *acquainted* with one another, or to have certainty of each other's existence, as standing in this attitude of accordance. For the thing itself carries confidence along with it. It enlarges the sphere of our reflective sympathy. This very plight of soul, wherein it rests at the determination to relinquish private wealth for *common* wealth whenever it meets with others of like views, implies such a degree of philanthropy and such an expansive liberality of mind as overlook all trivial obstacles to reposing confidence in others, and will place confidence in almost any human being that will listen to the reasoning by which it is generated: for none will patiently even *listen*, but such as have somewhat of congeniality of feeling herewith. This very plight of soul, I say, *makes* confidence, and guarantees its reciprocation: for it *excites* confidence; that is, it causes others to have confidence reciprocally, as soon as ever it makes itself perceived.

But how shall we find out those in whom we ought to place confidence, in order to make common stock of our private possessions without reserve?

I. I will in the first place endeavour to show what are *not* the effectual recourses to ascertain in whom we can place confidence. And,

First. It is not by looking about at the mere exterior appearances or circumstances of persons in a mixed concourse, to see what manner of countenances, dress, or air, they carry, nor by inquiring where they were born, on what patch of earth they have led their lives, nor indeed by knowing how they generally conduct themselves; even *this* is not a sure criterion.

Secondly. It is not by finding out what professions and declarations they make; for people have got the habit of speaking inadvertently and of speaking insincerely. They derive such habits from the circumstances of old society. They speak with a partial view of their subject; they have not fully felt all its bearings. They have inveterate habits which are at variance with what they say: and they have not so much as looked into a process of their eradication. Thus, we hear some warmly advocate the cause of the renovation, in *words*, saying they are friends, they are votaries of the social system; that all by nature have equal rights, that all products belong to all, that labor and enjoyment should be equal, &c. But bring them to the test, and immediately they begin to make excuses; they abandon their post. Herein they betray their ignorance of their own true interest, though they could conceive so clearly for others.

Thirdly. It is not always secure by fixing our view upon those who reason most clearly and forcibly upon this same subject, in a cold speculative way, in their closets or under circumstances which place them above the influence of those they address, or detach their interest altogether from the true weal of these. Thus we hear lawyers and divines often preach good morals, who themselves are exempt from practising their precepts.

Fourthly. It is not even by ascertaining that persons have borne heretofore a character of integrity, probity, or generosity—for two reasons: 1st—under the old institutions people act under a borrowed character: they are often obliged to appear what they are not. 2d. Fame is deceitful. It often happens that from wealth or power they get the character of being great and good, when they are not so. Popularity in the *old* world, is by no means the signal for confidence in the new.

Fifthly. We cannot always depend on their setting their names to an instrument of writing, binding them in their promise that they *will* conform to such and such rules, and that they will sink their private interest in the common interest, &c. For even here some will act deceitfully, bearing about them the characters they have drawn from the individual system; and promise things which they afterwards will not do.

We see then these are not the sure, effectual methods to avail ourselves of the criteria of a worthiness of confidence in order to a community of property.

II. I will proceed to endeavor to show what *are* the true methods and processes to ascertain in whom we can place confidence for such purpose. We shall make sure of this criterion when we find out those who have a congeniality of mind. Congeniality of mind comprehends similar feelings and similar reasoning. Similar reasoning leads to similar conclusions. Similar conclusions induce similar determinations: and when men coincide in this point, there is no great difficulty in the way of their co-operation.—In regard to this matter of bringing about a state of even and harmonious society, and coming back into the original order of our perfection as social intelligences, a train of reasoning from the true ground ultimately conducts us to the determination to yield up all our private possession, heretofore exclusive, whatever we may have, into a common stock when and wherever we meet with this coincidence and means of living in a state of association, for the express purpose of rendering every one alike comfortable as possible, in order to enlarge the compass of our own enjoyment of existence, [so far as any way derivable from matters of possession] by securing the good will, the good wishes, the approbation, and the assistance of all to each. Congeniality with this, is the desideratum we are in search of, when we would collect associates for a community of free men. Now for the means to detect this congeniality.

First. The first indication of it, is a patient and quiet auscultation to such reasoning as originally brings about this plight of mind. When one deliberately reasons clearly, step by step, from the true rudimental premises from which these truths are with certainty deduced— that is, from the homogeneity of our nature, its appetites, propensities, wants, affections, and passions, subject to the modification of exterior things with which it holds relations by the medium of its organs of perception, to the ultimate demonstrative conclusion, that for the happiness of human beings in a state of society to be the most extended and complete, there must be nothing exclusive, but all things must be common and inclusive, as much one's as another's; if persons listen with calm attention, with patience, and apparently an earnest desire to receive knowledge, they indicate some ground of confidence, as having this congeniality. This is the first degree of confidence we are induced to repose in them, in a view to the consummation which is the legitimate result of such trains of thought. For those who have no degree of this congeniality, will not patiently listen: they directly lean to some other object more entertaining, or they withdraw, with an intent pursuit of diversion. Such as listen intently, must be more or less interested in what they hear. Therefore this is an indication of that congeniality. This is a ground of reposing in them some degree of confidence.

Secondly. If they *acquiesce* in such reasoning; if they not only *listen* attentively, but evidently acquiesce in and assent to such reasoning, being apt to argue in precisely the same way themselves, we have still farther grounds for *another* and *higher* degree of confidence.— This is the second indication of congeniality of mind.

Thirdly. Another thing that gives evidence of this congeniality of mind, is the habit of consecutively making *professions* of this persuasion of mind, and declarative engagements to carry them to effect.—When they not only acquiesce in this scale of reasoning, but manifest a fixed determination to practise in conformity with it, by renouncing private wealth and adopting the state of common, undivided possession, participated in use according to need, we have reason to conclude that they are in a similar state of mind to that which qualifies them to be confidential associates in community of property. This gives ground to *another* degree of confidence, in this view.

Fourthly. When they not only *verbally* promise and resolve to put these principles into application, and to give themselves and all they possess to others of the same frame of mind, but freely put their names to a written compact that binds them to do it immediately, we have another indication of congeniality with this model, which propitiates a *higher* degree of confidence. At this point we may be almost *perfectly sure* that all such will make accessions to the union we are in pursuit of, and are fit associates.

Fifthly. When they actually *perform* what they have promised and are holden to by this compact or constitution, and without wavering or delay, render up all their private possessions if they have any, into a common stock, and devote their faculties to this very cause, proceed to concert measures for subsistence, and co-operate with those in the same plight, we have the last and complete indication of the congeniality we wish to find in all that we can make associates in community. This is the climax of the concludency, which demonstrates that worthiness of confidence in persons as co-operators and joint holders of what we have, or of the products of our labor. This completes the scale of criteria by which we know those in whom we can and ought to repose full confidence, as being worthy to be our associates and coadjutors, to be trusted, in common, with a free and equal use of what we now hold in exclusion, to whom we can give ourselves and all we possess, for the purpose of extending and refining the enjoyment of life.

For when persons not only listen attentively to this sort of reasoning that announces this state of mind and naturally leads to these determinations, but acquiesce in it and coincide with it; when they not only acquiesce in and practically adopt it, but verbally resolve and pledge themselves to conform to it in effect; when they not only enter into such engagement *verbally*, but put their names to written articles of compact with others, binding themselves to do so, i. e. to substitute common property for individual; when they not only profess, promise, engage, and bind themselves in writing, but actually *perform* what they have promised and are thus holden to, deliver up their private estates into a repository to serve at any time to supply the necessities of all their associates, and, whether they have any property or not, stand ready with their labor to promote by any kind of service the common cause; THEN all such minds, and every one that holds such train of reasoning, must necessarily have confidence in them as being congenial in their sentiments, their views, their determinations; as having a knowledge of the rights of human nature and the true interest of social mankind, and as being fit members of a union of free men in the order of our perfection and of the supreme good.

Now, then, when several persons are associated on these grounds, when they have placed their effects together in a common store for the benefit of all, [for example, three persons or more,] the course they aptly take, is to fix a rule by which they test all others that shall be admitted among them, that they shall enter, on the same terms, of retaining nothing exclusive, but giving full place to common property. They should have a scale of plain general precepts to regulate the movements of the whole. Included in their practical rules, is the provision for dismissal in case of a dereliction of the cause, as well as that they shall have liberty of absence when they please, and of withdrawal at any time, devoting all they possess to the cause, at the discretion of the majority. It is difficult to conceive a case of ten or twelve such persons collected together from such motives and to such an intent, who find it impossible to preserve their existence without abandoning their principles. For they can make their arrangements so that they might sojourn apart in case of unavoidable exigence of subsistence, without annulling their articles of coalition or impairing their mutual obligations. So far as they are sincere, and thorough converts, calamity will not be able to dissolve their union of hearts, even though it partially or temporarily disjoin their hands. When people are united in this way, upon the ground of a conscious congeniality of mind, coincidence of intentions, and knowledge of their own nature, they are not easily divided. There is a consent of feeling and a concurrence of action. They necessarily have a common interest.

The reason why I consider an actual willingness and readiness to sacrifice all private property to common property, to be the most important and main part of the proof of a man's character in point of qualifications for a community, is, that this is an adjunct of a degree of liberality and of magnanimity essential to such qualifi-

7

cations, which is not found to accompany any state of mind that falls short of this point. The superstitious have not arrived at it. The Shakers and Moravians are quoted as instances of rendering private wealth for common, but there is reason to believe they do it not from the heart, as free men; they do it under the pressure of some superstitious fear, hope, or admiration; they do it not altogether in the irresistible persuasion that it will infallibly increase their happiness as rational beings by gratifying a benevolent desire to make others equally happy as themselves, and thereby securing their good will. The avaricious and the vain have not arrived at it; and those who are eager for wealth, splendor, or celebrity.

Some have an argument that it is a matter of risk to resign private property and make it common stock with others. Many are of opinion that if they put their estates into a community's repository, they put it into a lottery. The noisy tone of society, in its present constitution, is sufficient to confuse the soundest minds, to interrupt their reasonings, to prevent their investigation. This argument I shall controvert. I contend there is not half the risk *here* that people run every day in *trading* under the laws of exclusive property. But to say they run a risk like that of putting money into a lottery, is absurd. I contend there is no such risk. 'While such suspicion of others and fear of the loss of property, infest the hearts of men, they have nothing like a community feeling; so far are they from being prepared to enter into the new order of society!'

As long as they consider a community to be a sort of lottery, in which every one that adventures any thing runs the chance of *losing* something, or a fellowship of trade where either all that enter put in equal shares of stock, or are estimated and privileged in the ratio of their respective shares, they are not capable of exemplifying the reality; they are not capable of a fair experiment—they have no heart for it—they are not true converts—they are deluded, or they go to practise delusion for some sordid designs, the success of which, will never exalt or refine their characters or meliorate the existing state of society. The communities of such men, are merely nominal. They are mere shadows of things ignorantly applauded, without the substance; or they illusively assume the name of that which they are not. They only re-exhibit what has been immemorially acted on the degenerate stage of human life by the sordid sons of avarice and trade. They lead back by a sure circuit into the exclusive systems of tyranny.

Now to the argument of a risk of losing property.

In the first place let us suppose thirteen persons associate on the principles above explained, putting in whatever estates they have, into one common treasury for constant use in proportion to the needs of all. One has a cow, another a horse, another a table and a dozen chairs, another one hundred bushels of corn, another a house and garden, another $100, &c., most of them having some value, to all which they quit every individual claim as in exclusion, and put it at the disposal of the whole; that they live regularly and quietly together one year; and that *then* twelve out of the thirteen unaccountably apostatize from the cause they have espoused, embezzle the whole of the property and run away with it, leaving the thirteenth alone and destitute, who still adheres to the cause. He has an action against them at common law, whether under the name of fraud, breach of covenant, robbery, or whatever other name; and before such a company of persons could clear themselves with their plunder, he *could* check their motion by a capias. But if his feelings revolted at a litigation, or they had sufficient address to escape, what would he have to regret? he had done that without which it is impossible for communities to exist; he finding it the duty of his life to support this cause by all in his power. What would he have to regret?

Secondly. What can a person lose, as an individual? He can lose what he owns. How much does one own? That which makes him comfortable; and nothing more. Every one owns, or has a right to, just so much as is effectual, in use, to make him comfortable as a sensible being and a reasonable being. If he has more than this, it does not belong to him. So, if one holds 10,000 dollars' value which he does not use, but has it in his pocket, or in his chest, or at interest, or in a storehouse, he does not own it; he does not rightfully possess it as an individual; it is not *his;* it does not belong to him by the law of right; it does not pertain to him, of *right*, by the original natural law of the perfection of human character and of human happiness in society. It belongs rather to those who lack a sufficient supply of their wants.— All that this man, then, would have lost as an individual, would be *his comfortable living in a community for the present moment.* This is the doctrine which those who set out to establish a real community espouse. Those who are prepared and capable to unite in a real community, admit this very doctrine, and build their constitution on it. This is the ground upon which those associates built the compacture of their society. It were very extraordinary indeed, and not to be expected, for twelve out of thirteen to suddenly abandon the principles they had enlisted to support: for they had acted from the *conviction* that the true standard of property, as applied to individuals, is WANT; and they go to follow the universal law of the preservation and perfection of the species; and not the temporizing and partial laws of political societies. This they have mutually pledged themselves to do, in all their dealings in reference to one another. Now it is extremely improbable that a majority will fall away in concert, and embezzle the whole estate.— Therefore there is little danger of the necessity or temptation to a lawsuit; for we have supposed the worst case: but should this happen, the individual who was left in adherence to the cause, would have a fair ground of a civil suit by the existing laws in this country, in Britain, and in Europe, by which he could not fail to succeed, if he were disposed to retrieve what he had added to the stock by resorting to the rules of the indi- vidual system to place himself on the same ground he stood on before. Thus, I say, in *this* sense there is little or no risk of the absolute deprivation of property.

One word more. It is pleaded by some, that it is not *prudent* for people to put in all they have at *first*, till they have made a fair trial of the community system, and seen whether men can live together in this way or not: it being a new experiment, lest it should fail a re- serve should be kept by those who can, for an emer- gency.

Be not deceived.—Rest assured of two things.

1. Every minute that associates live together in this way, they are receding farther and farther from that point of *mutual confidence* which shall induce them to make a common stock of their private property. At the end of a year they will be, if possible, less inclined to render up their private wealth than now; at the end of two years still less so. To indulge themselves in keep- ing hold on their peculiar accumulations while living together under the name of a community, is to corrupt, degrade, and finally obliterate the project; and to ex- tinguish all inclination towards such improvement.

2. Living in this way, is not living in a community.— Thus here is evident contradiction in this plea; it sup- poses an experiment to be made and *not* to be made.— When men hold private property at home or abroad, they do not live in a community. People that hold pe- culiar wealth exclusively to their names, whether in their pockets, in their chests, or abroad, are not mem- bers of a community. Living in this way, they make no experiment of the community system at all. In this way they will know as much about what a real community

is, twenty years hence, as they do now, and no more.—
In a real community, the members that compose it hold
no exclusive property on the face of the earth. There
is no community except where all detached private interests are sunk and confounded in *one common interest.*

To conclude. For those who are prepared for such
a sort of society, to enter fully into the order and pass
the remainder of their lives as a family, holding nothing
exclusive to the individual members, certainly cannot
have a tendency to interrupt the training of their children in a proper manner to the same end. Indeed it
must obviously serve rather to promote this very thing.
For while they experimentally know the benefits adjunct
to this order, they will with more alacrity conspire to
induct their offspring into it, to institute measures to perpetuate it, and with security to entail these benefits upon
succeeding generations, than when so far from realizing
any such result of the project, they remain even in doubt
of its practicability.

It was my intention to read, after the conclusion of
this discourse, a draught of a constitution for a community, the principal part of which was written some four
or five years ago, and which I had since considerably
enlarged. On my making a motion to proceed in this
reading, Mr. Owen recommended it as eligible to take
up the people's time in discussing what had been said,
rather than to charge their minds with too much matter
for contemplation at one time, and defer the reading of
the constitution to some other opportunity: to which I
implicitly acceded; when, Mr. Owen, remarking that he
had listened with critical attention, said, the principles
were unquestionable and the reasoning very good as re-
garded the theory, but that I entirely 'overlooked the
practice,' or 'what was necessary to the practice:' [be-
hold! the practice was the very thing I had been talking
about:] and went on to observe that I "forgot" or "overlooked" how imprudent it would be, and not to be ex-

pected of any persons having wealth, to make it common stock with a parcel of people with whom they were not acquainted, and in whom they could not repose confidence. To which I opportunely retorted, that he "overlooked" that it was on these very principles, *intimate acquaintance* and *mutual confidence*, that I had supposed persons to associate together, making common property; that it was on this very supposition that the persons had the utmost grounds of confidence in one another in this view, that they *had* this confidence, and from *this cause* they associated themselves together and made their property common stock, that I had made my instance. From this he went on to make some other observations to the people; and Mr. Evans and some others making their remarks and putting queries, there was some conversation that perhaps was interesting, but did not lead to any very interesting conclusion.— The next day I proposed to read my constitution at night, either before or after Mr. Owen's school exercises. Having given notice accordingly, I read that paper to a numerous assembly immediately after those ceremonies were concluded, about 8 o'clock in the evening. The next morning (September 12th) I took up my residence in the boarding school, in the dominions of the education society, being employed in the occupation of teaching; where I have remained ever since.

Hearing that persons objected to some few articles, I gave notice, a day or two after, that I would meet all those who mostly acquiesced in the principles of that constitution, the next Sunday morning, in the Hall, at 8 or 9 o'clock, and answer all objections, endeavor to satisfactorily explain, and prove the consistency and practicability of every article. Accordingly, attending seasonably at the time mentioned, there was no regular audience to me; but only a few scattering persons talking in groups. Therefore I deferred this vindication till evening; when, after Mr. Owen's exercising his scholars,

and making an address to the people, reading a newspaper, &c., I proceeded to fulfil my engagement. A respectable number remained to hear, Mr. Owen and the
multitude having withdrawn. Here the constitution had
a second reading, and some comments. These people
generally acquiesced in it, and no serious objection was
brought forward against any clause. It was recommended to me, and agreed among some of these people,
that another meeting should be appointed to be held
on Tuesday night following, at the shoe factory or tobacco factory, where a discourse should be delivered
and some plan and measures discussed for the application of our principles to practice. Now the chamber of
the tobacco factory was the place where the mechanics'
society were used to hold their deliberative meetings,
and that of ·the shoe factory was then used for Owen's
school. It was said by one of these mechanics, there
would be no difficulty in obtaining either of these buildings for a meeting. This appointment was therefore
made, the people present depending on such meeting at
the time and place mentioned; and, it growing late, we
all retired. Seeing but few persons were present at the
appointment of my meeting, I thought it would be proper
and necessary to put up a notification, which therefore
the next day I did, in the following form, on the wall of
the inn where such papers were used to be posted.

" A meeting of the REPUBLICANS of New-Harmony and
its vicinity, is to be held to-morrow evening, at 7 o'clock
precisely, over the shoe factory [if attainable,] or otherwise in the tobacco factory, where a discourse will be
delivered, plans discussed, and modes and measures in-
vestigated for a practical application of their principles.
A general attendance is expected.
"New-Harmony, September 19, 1826."

This paper had not remained in·that place two hours
before Mr. Owen tore it down. In walking I missed it,

and asked a young man who came running towards me who tore it down? he said, "Mr. Owen; and he wants to see you." Mr. Owen soon met me, and, somewhat angrily expostulating with me as if I had not obtained the *consent of the societies,* observing such a thing could not be done without it, said it was wrong, would make disturbance, &c. yet never returning me the paper. The next day as I was walking through town, about the eleventh hour, Owen met me, saying, 'Paul Brown what are you doing?' Not being accustomed to such manner of salutation of a sudden while walking, I was a little at a loss how to reply at once: but after some hesitation, I brought out, in my quaker way, *'keeping school.'* 'Aye? where?' *'At the boarding school. Why? for what did you want to know what I am doing?'* 'Because any one that is in no regular business, has no right to stay here.' After a little, he asked me if I were a member? saying, 'any one who is not a member of any society, has no right to be here.' Notwithstanding it was a well known fact that a number of persons were employed in town on wages, who were not members and did not wish to be; besides, different persons in all the societies were only visitors, or living upon sufferance, or trial, not know-ing whether they should be members or not: and more than all this, the people of the mechanics' and pastoral societies were, strictly, *none* of them members. He began speaking of the advertisement, saying it was very wrong to put up such papers,—I maintaining it was *not* wrong for me to invite people to meet, when requested by people of the place to hold a meeting; besides, one had a right to invite a meeting in any town in the United States, whether requested or not, and if people assem-bled they could hold their debates in the highway if no room could be obtained, unless they chose to disperse. He said it was contrary to the rules of the societies. Now, no such rules existed in any of the societies. He spoke of my poverty; saying, 'because *you* are poor, you want those that have wealth, to make common property.' He mentioned an instance of my necessity of borrowing, and said, 'if you cannot provide support for *yourself*, how could you contrive means for the maintenance of eight or ten persons?' [or words to this effect;] alluding, no doubt, to some design he suspected or imagined I had, to attempt the founding of a community, which might draw some people from under *his* hammer and tongs. So then, here, this Mr. Robert Owen, who had publicly denounced individual property as one of the heads of that hydra which had hatched all the crimes and miseries of society, makes it the criterion of a man's worth, and depreciates one's character in proportion to the lack of it. This is not the only instance in which this man has exemplified a contempt of poverty, and deference for the indications of wealth and success.

Towards evening I posted another notification to the same effect, by the gateway of the boarding school [this being out of Owen's dominions,] and the other buildings being bolted against us, we held our meeting in the school room of Mr. Neef, where, after a discourse was delivered, the constitution had a third reading and some discussion.

Now in this week's Gazette [of September 13,] appeared the following notice in review of the events of the preceding Sunday.

"Instead of the usual morning Sunday meeting, Paul Brown requested to be allowed to deliver a lecture on the formation of communities, and this gave rise to an animated and interesting discussion."

Thinking that this must have proceeded from some oversight, and judging it as likely as otherwise to have slipped from some other pen than Owen's, I handed forward the following note for insertion in the succeeding number of the paper.

Messrs. Editors—

In your last appears to be a small mistake relating to the business of Sunday morning. Instead of requesting to be allowed to deliver a lecture on the formation of communities, no such request was made at all, [neither perhaps ought to be supposed that in a republic or any thing claiming the title, one person rather than another should have to request as a special privilege to be *allowed* to deliver his thoughts in any way;] but it having been ascertained that no person intended to occupy the Hall for any other purpose at that hour, an appointment was made, and notice given three days previous, not that a lecture would be delivered on the *formation of communities*, [no particular subject being named;] whereupon a number of persons, being assembled together at the hour mentioned, gave audience to a discourse, not exactly on the formation of communities, but an investigation of the grounds of mutual confidence in persons, to a degree sufficient to make a common stock of all their private or individual property without reserve: *then*, to be sure, what had therein been said, gave rise to some discursive confabulation.

P. BROWN.

This paper being put into the hands of the printer, and he having delivered it seasonably to Mr. Owen, never was seen nor heard from again by me. Happily I had retained its duplicate.

In the course of this same week, notifications were set up, of a great and general assembly of all the societies and the whole population of the town, at the Hall, on the next Sunday, when some one of the prodigious plans of amelioration that had been hatched or brewed, was to be brought upon the carpet. On the morning of this next Sunday, then, being the 17th of September, the multitudes flocked to the Hall from all the Societies, and a numerous throng congregated there before 10 o'clock;

though the day being cloudy and cool, not many ladies were present. After some bickering carping between the heads or leaders of the different societies, by way of disputing about the existence of a jealous and suspicious disposition in either society towards other, each claiming the honor of a peaceable and harmonious character, and it having been proclaimed that the object of the meeting was to explore some method to improve the condition of the people, make them more contented, &c., and all being invited to suggest any expedient they could think of towards such end, [with a most solid assurance, no doubt, that there was no one that would speak a word;] one General somebody *letting the cat out of the bag*, as the saying is, [which in this instance proved to be no more than an owl with twelve claws,] stood up on the stage and read a message from Mr. Owen, who was aloof, holding forth stipulations to enter into a community with as many as would join him, himself to be a member; every member to put in all his property; EXCEPT what he thought might be necessary to reserve to help his friends, [in short, whatever he pleased to reserve;] to have an *energetic government*, to consist of himself and four others of his choice, to be appointed by him every year; the government not to be altered for five years; property to be appraised; members to withdraw when they please, but not to take away their property in less than five years, except the interest on it, which they are to commence drawing at whatever time they leave the society; Owen and the men of his choice to have the sole direction of all the business and arrangements, &c. On the evening of the next day, they held another meeting and sat late, when all persons that chose, or that had any disposition to join Owen, from either of the societies, attending, they agreed upon the new government. General Evans, lawyer Clark, Wm. Owen, and J. Schnee, were the persons nominated and appointed to help govern. They, in conjunction with

Mr. Owen, were to have unlimited absolute power over the affairs of the society, which was to be called New-Harmony community No. 1. An invitation was sent to communities No. 2 and No. 3, to join, and throw in their estates into the common stock. Poor Macluria, or No. 2, being convulsed by jealousies and party feelings on account of some being religious and some few not, and some disagreement about their distributions and arrangements, was likely to be an easy prey, as the fawn between the tyger and lion was to the fox.

The next Sunday [Oct. 1st] was the day appointed for the exhibition of the propounded compact, and offering it for signatures. Many assembled on that day, and among others several members of the aforesaid neighboring communities. The instrument was read. It was sharper than the outline had indicated. Mr. Owen took a vote of the people, a ceremony that was customary with him, of their willingness that he should rule! The paper was lodged at the tavern for signatures. After the finishing stroke of its revision, it stood as follows:

We who have set our hands and seals to the following covenant and agreement, believing that human happiness can be greatly increased by a number of individuals uniting themselves into a society or community of equality, where the rights and duties of all are reciprocal, where labor is united and property held in common, have, for the attainment of these objects as far as the present state of society will justify, united ourselves into a society or community, to be known among ourselves by the name of New-Harmony community No. 1, and subscribed this covenant or agreement, as forming the fundamental articles of our association.

1. Each of the undersigned individuals hereby obligate and bind themselves, severally to convey, for the use of all the parties to these presents, all their estates both real and personal, in the UNITED STATES, EXCEPT WHAT MAY BE SUFFICIENT TO PAY THEIR JUST DEBTS, THEIR

WEARING APPAREL, HOUSEHOLD FURNITURE, AND WHAT THEY MAY FEEL DISPOSED TO SET APART FOR THE ASSISTANCE AND SUPPORT OF ABSENT RELATIVES WHO ARE NOT MEMBERS OF THE COMMUNITY. The real estate to be conveyed to the parties to these presents, shall be a leasehold estate of ten thousand years; all of which property when so conveyed, together with all property that may be accumulated by the parties to these presents during the time their names may remain annexed hereto, shall be known and considered as the common stock of said community, subject to the conditions hereinafter provided.

2. For the management of the property conveyed as above provided, and all other property accumulated by the parties hereto, together with all the concerns of the society, it is agreed that Robert Owen shall, for the term of five years, [except as hereinafter provided] annually appoint four others that are parties to this agreement, who, together with himself, shall form a board of trustees. These trustees shall have the SOLE MANAGEMENT AND CONTROL OF SAID PROPERTY; shall make rules and regulations for the society; shall admit persons to become parties hereto, and shall erase the name of any individual when in their opinion the good of the society may require; and all decisions made and acts done by the authority of a majority of said trustees, shall be considered and taken as the decisions and acts of the whole: provided, the first four persons thus to be appointed, shall be Robert M. Evans, Amos Clark, William Owen, and John Schnee.

3. In case of the death, voluntary resignation, or removal of any trustee above provided for, the remaining trustees shall appoint some person to fill such vacancy; and the person thus appointed, shall have and exercise the same power as the person whose vacancy he fills.

4. Any member holding any agency or office, such as trustee or otherwise, on having his name erased from this agreement, shall from thence cease to have or ex-

ercise any power or authority by virtue of such agency, and his situation as such shall be considered vacant.

5. Persons may from time to time, by and with the consent of the trustees, become parties to this agreement, and individuals at their own request shall have their names erased herefrom; and such addition or erasure shall in no wise destroy or alter the force and effect of this agreement between those whose names remain subscribed; and any failure of an individual in the full performance of all the covenants herein contained, shall not release others from a full and faithful observance of the same on their part.

6. All property conveyed or accumulated by the parties to or in pursuance of this agreement, shall be occupied by the parties hereto as joint tenants; provided, however, that no individual shall have such interest therein as ever to enable him or her, or any person for him or her or to his or her use, to sell, dispose of, or sever the same from others; but the sole interest that any individual shall have in the same, shall consist in the use thereof for his or her support and maintenance during the time such individual continues a party to this agreement, except as hereafter provided.

7. Each individual on making the conveyance of property for the benefit of the parties hereto as herein provided, shall receive from the trustees a certificate for the same, stating the kind, quantity, and value of the property thus conveyed, and the time and manner the same is liable to be refunded; and such individual, on having his or her name erased from this agreement, shall have the same property or other of a similar kind equal in value, at the option of the trustees, restored in ten days after it is demanded, if the amount thus conveyed and demanded does not exceed five hundred dollars; but all sums over and above that amount shall be restored or paid for in manner above provided, in annual instalments of one thousand dollars each after it is demanded,

unless the amount so conveyed and deposited shall exceed twenty thousand dollars, in which case the same shall be restored or paid for in twenty equal annual instalments after it is demanded; but no demand shall be made for the restoration or payment of property thus conveyed except to the amount of five hundred dollars, within five years after such conveyance or deposite is made: provided, however, that any individual having his or her name erased from this agreement, shall be intitled to have interest on the amount of the property so conveyed or deposited, at the rate of 5 per cent., paid semi-annually in advance when demanded, but no interest shall be paid for the time such person's name remains to this agreement.

8. That no part of the property conveyed by an individual or accumulated by the united exertions of the parties to these presents in pursuance of this agreement, shall ever go to the heirs, executors, administrators, or assigns of any persons making such conveyance or deposite, but the interest of every such individual shall go at his decease to the other persons whose names are annexed to this agreement, to be by them disposed of in the following manner, viz.—if such deceased person leaves a wife, she shall be entitled to become a party to this agreement and shall have placed to her credit and have a certificate for one-third of the amount conveyed or deposited by her deceased husband; and shall be entitled to draw the same out as other persons making conveyances or deposites, and the other two-thirds shall be placed in equal proportions to the credit of the children, if any, of such deceased persons, who as they arrive at the age of twenty-one years, shall have the same control over the amount placed to their credit, and it shall be subject to the same rules, as if deposited by themselves at the time of their becoming parties to this agreement or arriving at the age of twenty-one years.

9. The widows of deceased husbands shall be treated kindly, and their minor children shall enjoy the same privileges during their minority, if they continue in the society, as the children of living members.

10. Persons having their names erased from this agreement at their own request or otherwise as herein provided, shall be entitled to no compensation for services, but shall thereby abandon all claim to property belonging to the parties to these presents, except the amount of their deposite; and shall thereby be discharged from all liability to pay money by reason of any of the covenants herein contained: provided that the trustees shall have power to make such allowance to individuals leaving the society as they may think right and just, taking into consideration the means and ability of the society and benefits received from such persons.

11. Within the three months next preceding the expiration of the five years in which said Robert Owen has the power of appointing trustees, a majority of the parties to these presents shall agree in what manner the business of the society shall in future be conducted, and how and in what manner and in whom the powers hereby delegated to said trustees shall be vested, and shall sign a covenant to that effect; and any of the parties refusing to sign said covenant after it is signed by the majority, shall have their names erased from this agreement.

12. In addition to the foregoing provisions, persons shall be liable to have their names erased from this agreement for the following causes, viz. unreasonable absenting themselves from the society without leave, intemperance, dishonesty, wastefulness, negligence, unkindness, unfriendly and harsh treatment to their fellow members or others. And as this society is formed for the purpose of rendering the situation of its members as comfortable and happy as their means will permit,

all the undersigned individuals obligate and bind themselves to use their best endeavors by temperate, economical, and prudent habits, to contribute to the interest of all and the happiness of each.

In testimony whereof we have hereunto set our hands
and seals this 2d day of October, 1826.

Here followed the names, first, of Robert Owen, next
those of the other trustees, and afterwards the names
of other persons. And it is a well known fact that this
same Mr. Robert Owen did put his name to such an
agreement, whereof the foregoing is a true copy, and
that the other four men of his choice and appointment,
as trustees, did likewise put *their* names to the same
instrument, as well as several other persons who afterwards followed the example. After a few days it was
said to have ninety names. Such was the government
adopted, such was the state of things, in the second week
of October. This superseded and trampled under foot
all the indentures, deeds, leases, and bonds, that conveyed property to the farmers and mechanics. We shall
see, by and by, what came to pass four months afterwards. It had been reported that the mechanics' and
farmers' societies had, to a man, joined themselves to
Mr. Owen's standard, acceding to the new government:
but, it was only a *part* of what had verbally and nominally joined, that would *sign* the compact when it made
its full appearance: therefore this was a time of disper-
sion; like, in some degree, that which succeeded the
division; and many began to prepare to take their leave
of the stage of New-Harmony. Two men from the
society of education went and joined themselves to
No. 1, signing the compact: they soon wished themselves back, but could not so easily return. The remainder of the education society continued steady at
their business, entertaining but a low opinion of this
new government: some called it an oligarchy; others

a limited monarchy; others again, an obsolute despotism. It was reported that Robert Dale Owen, belonging to this society of education, was, sans ceremonie,
appointed treasurer, and editor of the Gazette, for this
new community No. 1, and was attached to this and
detached from the other without ever moving his residence. The old man, too, immediately took up his
abode with him in the palace of No. 5, directly after
the establishing of this compact. He was ill, and discontinued preaching and keeping school; so that his
school rather declined, and dwindled away.

In the course of this week, well aware that no such
sentiments would be admitted into the Gazette, nor
especially any thing from *my* pen, I set up a sheet on
the boards by the side of our gateway, containing the
following observations, that the people might read it at
their leisure. For besides its being exposed to all the
population, as they chanced to pass that way, the whole
of this education society, which was then quite numerous, constantly ate in our dining hall. It begins with
an allusion to an argument that had been held by some
persons, of the necessity of individual indemnification
in case of making community of property.

"This argument of the fear of the want of confidence
to *take place hereafter*, or rather a fear that the majority
will not do justice, is in open contradiction with what
has been admitted, that [of persons compacting conscientiously on the conviction of universal equality]
every one has confidence in every other, all having
associated on an assurance of congeniality in the persuasion of the only base of a commonwealth. These
things being supposed to be real, [no matter whether
there are few persons or many,] and a constitution and
rules agreed on, which shall gage the characters of all
that *shall* belong to the society, where this confidence
is, THIS FEAR CANNOT BE. It contradicts and excludes it.
To fear that one will be unjust or unreasonable, is to *not*

have *full confidence* in him. To have full confidence in one, presupposes that he has stability. It implies an assurance that he has stability. Therefore, if one is so fearful that the majority of those he associates with, will be unreasonable and unjust, and not give him what is actually reasonable if ever he shall voluntarily or forcedly leave them, as to require or wish a guarantee of the amount of what he adds to the wealth of the society by stock or labor, with interest, he thereby PROVES that he has not full confidence in those associates, and thus is not prepared to enter into a commonwealth, not heartily and unreservedly embracing the rudimental principle; therefore, is not a fit associate. Such may form copartnerships, fellowships of trade, associations for co-operative labor, canal and bridge companies, banking associations, &c.; but a community or republic of free, rational, enlightened persons, is another thing.

"The idea of a loss of individual property, belongs to a speculation that precludes a community feeling. Those who associate together in community of property, [being rational,] do so because they have a conviction and mutual assurance of a concurrence in the conviction of this truth as matter of demonstrative certainty, that no man owns, of right, any thing more than what makes him comfortable, every one having alike a right to a supply of his wants; and admitting this, they must admit [what irresistibly follows] that therefore if one has a hoard of superfluous wealth, he cannot lose it because it is not *his;* it belongs to those who have not enough: [and a man cannot lose what does not belong to him, any more than an oyster can climb an appletree.] He that has a different view of this, still adheres to the system of exclusive property. He denies the doctrine of commonwealths. This must be self-evident. For a fear of the loss of individual property in superfluity held in exclusion, proves that a person having such fear has not renounced private property and given the prefe-

rence to *common* property, but still clings to his private
peculiar interest. He reckons upon private property
and sets a value on it. He considers it necessary to his
happiness. This is contradictory and exclusive of his
acquiescing in the proposition of universal equality of
rights. If a man says *he is afraid he shall lose his private
wealth*, he proves he is no community man. He proves
at once that he prefers private property to common
property; that he prefers to shirk in the way of individual fortune, to sharing in the common lot with others.
The idea of individual loss, is wholly contradictory of
assent to the proposition that none has any true property but of what is necessary and sufficient to satisfy his
wants and make him comfortable. Those who are
thorough converts to this, will not desire to live on a
private fortune by themselves after once living in the
TRUE ORDER. They certainly will choose rather to range
about, exploring congenial minds and such as dare
uphold their tenets.

"A community that moils in trade, exemplifies but
little advancement in civilization beyond the present
general character of mankind, it keeping up the self-
same practices and habits that characterize the most
degenerate stage of society.

"A community of persons having for their sole object
to accumulate wealth, and who starve themselves for
the sake of getting rich, is not a worthier model than a
miserly or selfish person who hides his treasures in
the earth.

"A community of sharpers is no better than an individual sharper.

"To enjoy the life of a philosopher, is to be free from
all mercantile calculation. Not to be addicted to mercantile calculation, is to have superseded it by a different course of measures for attaining all the assurances
among those which this is instituted to secure, that are
necessary to the enjoyment of life. To be averse to

such things, and to have an opposite habit of thinking, is to discontinue the practice of that sort of speculation. To discontinue any practice, destroys the habit of that practice. Nothing will eradicate a mercantile disposition, with all the ill feelings that generate from it, but a discontinuance of mercantile practices. The way to perpetuate it, is to continue and refine the arts of trade, and keep an example of such practices constantly before the eyes of the rising generation."

This paper stood posted in that place three or four days, being taken in at nights, lest it should be purloined or destroyed. But, for any utility of its effect, I might as well have set it up on the inside of Newgate; for even there it might have caught the eye of many an honest generous hearted fellow.

About this time Mr. William M'Clure arrived from sojourning in Ohio. I think his arrival was on the evening of the 6th of October. He was pleased with what the education society had accomplished by their industry in their out-door work; but was very much controlled in his estimate of the school by the influence of those who were adverse to the main institution and to the union of the society.

Owen's illness was short, but he still continued at No. 5, occupying one room, the editor another, M'Clure another, and Madame Fratageot others; none of those dwelling here being members of the society, but mostly such as were opposed to its existence.

The people having fitted up a large brick and stone granary for an eating-room, removed from the boarding school and took their meals in the granary, none but the children and teachers remaining to eat at the school house.

As I observed before, R. D. Owen was henceforth the editor of the Gazette, and his father no longer nominally so; though this last being the lord proprietor of the press, and having absolute dominion wherever he had property and influence, reserved to himself as it were a negative upon certain sorts of writing, or the power of excluding and inserting what he pleased. Nevertheless, there was little sign of clashing between these, they coinciding very exactly in their views of personal aggrandizement, and suspicion of whatever could be construed into a reflection on their morals. They seemed to have abandoned the principles of the prospectus of their paper, and to be governed rather more by favoritism than by those. They chose to keep on the sure side of the hedge, as the saying is, and, like the priesthood, took care to publish 'every thing on one side of the question and nothing on the other,' except where they knew they were able to vindicate themselves, with advantage, making a show of victory. Not 'all that was true,' not all that was 'expressed in good feeling and good sense,' could now gain admittance into this paper, nor even what accorded with the most important of their own professed opinions, if it happened to come from such as they deemed *their enemies*: but what came from their particular friends and favorites and persons at a distance, who being in delusion about the state of things here and the motives of those that ruled, could be made friends, at least were not likely to be enemies, was the first and foremost on their files. Several delusive misrepresentations of the state of things here went abroad in the Gazette, of which hundreds of persons could attest the very reverse to be the matters of fact. It had been stated, among other things, that the children were improved in their minds and morals; the contrary of which was daily seen and felt: for it was a noted fact that their morals grew worse instead of better; and that no other place was known in the United States that had a set of children equally numerous collected in the like compass, that were of so harsh, insolent, rash, boisterous, and barbarous dispositions. It was also repeatedly set forth or insinuated, that we were making rapid progress in the practice of the new system, were in a fair way of consolidating our community, and were waxing in social feelings; but not a word was said of the trading, the indentures, the leases, the bonds, the conveyances, the rents, the bargain-making, and the bargain-breaking. Though it must be acknowledged, that when the son came to have the conducting of the paper, there was somewhat more of candour in relating the things of this place, than when it was altogether in the hands of the father.

No. 2, or Macluria, split into two parties nearly equal. Those of the one to which it was left to pay off the incumbrances on the inheritance, such as interest and principal to Owen, and the worth of their services and productions to the other party, or leave and *be paid*, concluding themselves unable, gave up, and withdrew to their farms in the country; whereupon the others taking the whole burden on themselves, immediately threw it off, by relinquishing and rendering back the whole property into the hands of Mr. Owen. Thus this estate of 1200 acres, with their houses, &c. was swallowed up in No. 1; and a part of those who remained, soon after removed to New-Harmony: this happened in November. About the 7th of that month a report came about that Mr. Owen, despairing of taking the school society and bringing them under his wing by stratagem or force, resorted to methods to starve them to a surrender, by cutting off all supplies; refusing to sell, even for money.— After a day or two, however, he had the compassion to permit them to continue purchasing goods at his store.

A short communication was sent to the press, designed for the Gazette, (while Mr. Owen was editor,) by a friend of the reformation, particularly recommendatory of the plan of overturning the system of monopoly and exclusion, and never was seen nor heard from again by those concerned.

As Mr. Owen was still supposed to retain in his charge

four of the six papers that I had sent him, and they
having remained in that posture six or seven weeks,
without any reply from him whether he had examined
or intended to print them or not; I wishing to arrange
my papers, addressed him the following lines:

*New-Harmony, October* 21, 1826.
Sir—If you recollect, six numbered pieces, of those
which had been presented for the Gazette, were handed
you by Mr. Pelham for your examination; two of which
have since been published. It is desirable [for certain
reasons] to know before long whether you have thoroughly and satisfactorily examined the remainder of
those pieces, and whether thereupon you have determined to publish them in the Gazette or to reject them.
Respectfully, &c. P. BROWN.

To this he made me no reply; and never mentioned
the subject when he saw me afterwards, any more than
if I had been a dog. Two or three weeks afterwards,
I stopped at the editor's room to inquire about these
things; in the mean time I had presented a communication by way of asking explanation of a passage in a reply between some correspondents that disputed on certain religious or theological questions, which now was
returned to me rejected, [it being thought it might puzzle
or embarrass the disputants,] together with two of the
four papers before mentioned, I asking for a return of all
those things which they did not intend to publish. The
remaining two were to appear in the next papers. In
the course of six weeks they made their appearance.—
Soon after, I presented another paper, which by the way
was brief and not repetitious, to keep up the series till
something could be said about the practical cultivation
of the ARTS in a commonwealth; it being a subject that
had not been analytically eventilated. This it seems
was rejected altogether, it being returned to me, on my

inquiring about it seven weeks afterwards, with no other reason given for its refusal but that it was written in an old style; which indeed was the same style as all my former communications were written in. From this time forth, finding their press was less free than some others in the country, I troubled them with no more communications for the public.

Mr. Owen, as soon as his health was sufficiently restored, recommenced his preaching, but not his school. On Sunday, the 12th day of November, he came forth and delivered in the Hall a lengthy discourse, saying, in effect, among other things, that no person was to blame for any thing he did or might do, any more than another person. From this day forth, his preaching was a regular course of Sabbath sermonizing; being a series of chapters called the 'social system,' which came out regularly in the Gazette, after reading or delivering in the Hall. In one of these, [I think the 3d chapter, No. 15, of volume 2d of the Gazette,] he has this passage:

"It having been discovered that man at birth is wholly formed by the power which creates him, and that his subsequent character is determined by the circumstances which surround him, acting upon his original or created nature; that he does not in any degree form himself, physically or mentally, and therefore cannot be a free or responsible agent; the first practical effects of this knowledge must be to banish from the mind of man all IDEAS OF MERIT OR DEMERIT in any CREATED OBJECT OR BEING; TO EXTIRPATE FROM HIS CONSTITUTION ALL THE FEELINGS TO WHICH SUCH IDEAS GIVE RISE; and thus at once to reconcile him to human nature, to himself, and to all his fellow creatures."

This doctrine, of no praise nor blame, no merit nor demerit, no reward nor punishment, [called artificial if instituted,] in effect no moral right nor wrong, and, as it were, no virtue nor vice, no black nor white, had visibly a demoralizing effect upon the promiscuous multitude to which it was addressed. Forsooth, what effect could most rationally be expected of such doctrine as this, rammed down the throats of inexperienced boys and girls, inconsiderate, dull, illiterate men and silly women? Was it not eminently fitted to sweep from the human heart, as with the blazoned besom of extermination, the *ens insitus* of every principle of virtuous morals of which it could be the subject?

On the evening of the 23d of November, a log dwelling house, uninhabited, [near the rope walk,] was burnt to the ground, from boys going in with torches, to rob beehives which were lodged there.

On the 25th, M'Clure retired, pursuing his travels to New-Orleans: moreover he left a younger brother who had recently arrived from the south, as a sort of steward and treasurer, to act in his stead in adverting to the maintenance of the establishment.

Mr. Owen's school failing, his young teachers were directed to conduct their pupils to No. 5, every day, [instead of the Hall,] where they had most of their scholastic exercises; till he negotiated to enter twenty boys at the boarding school as formerly, to be taught on the Pestalozzian plan; detaining the balance to attend No. 5, under Madame Fratageot. In effect he sent twenty-two. These twenty-two boys fell to my charge. They commenced their attendance November 28th, being conducted daily to my room by one of their tutors.—From dwelling with their parents, and only being exercised in memory, as about geography, in their schooling, they not only had lost, by three months' absence, what they had once gained in scientific attainments in their former attendance here; but, still lodging at their homes, were even more harsh, volatile, incorrigibly refractory, and insolent, than those that had kept their abode here: so that it was evident they had not profited in the way of cultivation of temper and morals.

To revert to the politics of No. 1.—This new REGIME:

of course tumbled to the ground the throne of the trium-
virate or trinity of the mechanics; and a government by
FIVE, of paramount 'energy,' rode upon its ruins. Let
us have a glance at their administration, and see what
manner of rule they held. Many people left the town
when this mockery of a social compact was adopted;
and in fact most of those who signed it, did so for con-
venience, till they might have opportunity to remove;
chief of them being poor and unable to get any other
place at the present moment, unless there were some
slavish souls who could passively submit to despotism;
but the most of the commonwealth men were gone clear,
except what dwelt in the education society. If there
were two or three real republicans unable to do better,
they were painfully sensible of the disgraceful manner
in which they were controlled. In short, the inhabitants
of Owen's dominions were a discontented race, full of
complaints, and always with some reason; suffering privations, neglect, and delusion; given to distrust, suspicion, ill feelings, backbiting, reproach, calumny. Here,
as in all parts of the town from the beginning, was a peculiar lack of sympathy, by reason of individual suffering. The sustenance was dealt out in scanty rations on
set days. Partiality found its way into this distribution.
Some favorites and the families of trustees were indulged
with conveniences, [whether of clothing or provision,]
which other laboring, drudging poor were denied upon
asking. By some accounts, the new cabinet ruled like
star-chamber; their decrees being dictated by their feelings, and *their* judgment of *general opinion*, without much
balancing of external evidence, except the *paper* evidence of mercantile computations; but above all things,
setting aside their scrupulous feelings of dignity, their
account book was their statute code. Looking on paper, they decided people's characters by the dollars and
cents set against their names by way of debt or credit.
He that *consumed* more than he *produced*, according to

the prices *they* had instituted to be set upon both services and maintenance, was to be turned out of the society.— Many were the wrongs of individuals. Some were turned out with scarce a minute's warning. The overseers, intendants, and trustees, were inexperienced and unskilful in the business they directed others upon doing, whence arose dissatisfaction, and suspense; every thing was in uncertainty; every thing went wrong; nothing prospered; nothing was successful. A gardener, named Gilbert, who, being of an occupation that was not very productive in the winter and not much in demand, happened to be in the rear upon the books, in other words, he and his family being discovered to *consume more than they produced*, as the saying was, and some person or persons having reported to the trustees that he was idle, lazy, negligent, &c., had his discharge sent him of a sudden, when his family was sick, in the extremity of winter. Whereafter this Mr. Gilbert, who by the way was well known to be an active, faithful, and diligent man in his occupation, having obtained of the education society the privilege of the Hall for this purpose, invited all the inhabitants of the town, with his accusers, to meet there on Sunday, the 31st of December, in order for an investigation of this subject, whether the ostensible grounds of his dismissal were true or false: at which time the people to a considerable number having assembled, it being a cold blustering day, the investigation, though a little retarded by Mr. Owen's talking, at last went on regularly; and, no accusers appearing to maintain the imputation that had been laid on him, and it appearing by evidence that the contrary was true, it was recorded that the charge was unfounded, false, and calumnious and that Mr. Gilbert had the character of being an industrious citizen: so that the man came off with "flying colors," as the saying is; or, as *another* saying is, " came out like gold purified seven times;" although he was no longer a member of the society, and did not wish to be.

But let us turn aside from this scene of wretchedness and uproar in the south part of the town, and see what has been hatched in the cabinet of the royal palace at No. 5. Mr. Owen, it seems, having reunited the domain of Macluria to his own, had an object to enlarge his dominions as much as possible, and was very desirous to effect a combination of the whole school society with his No. 1, in which failing, he was anxious to get back some of the land [particularly the best] to attach to the other estate, to straighten some lines, make the estate more valuable, &c., and ultimately reclaimed a certain part on the alleged ground of a misunderstanding. The education society refused to relinquish any, were determined to adhere to their contract, and admitted no misunderstanding about the matter. Now, as was before related, about 900 acres of land, more or less, with several valuable buildings, had been legally conveyed to this society by a lease of ten thousand years instead of a deed, the greatest part of the pay being advanced to Owen by M'Clure, [at least much more than the value of all the land] wherefore the lease was assigned to *him:* so that the society were to make their payments to said M'Clure: whether to him or Owen, not a cent was yet due, for six months to come. Rather the greatest part of this land lay low and was subject to inundation almost every year. No interest was due till the end of the first year; which had not come about. This land had certain boundaries. Mr. Owen's own son, the present editor of the Gazette, was the man who surveyed or run out the land. The lines were perspicuously laid down in the body of the lease. After mature deliberation, and a clear understanding on both sides, Mr. Owen put his name with his own hand, under the lease. Still he was dissatisfied without having some of the land restored to his control: and in the Gazette of Nov. 29, No. 9, Vol. 2, appeared in the editor's department the following remarks, which were said to come from the pen of Mr. Owen the elder.

"Another cause of some dissatisfaction among the members of the education society arose from misconception among them as to the best line of separation between their lands and those of the other societies. They thought some other line, giving them more land in a particular direction inconvenient to their neighbors, was necessary for them: however, a little reflection will convince them of this error, there being more land than is requisite for ten other communities; and whenever they are prepared to require more for cultivation, it can be obtained without any difficulty. It deserves not a moment's consideration whether one society has a little more or a little less land at the present, provided a line shall be adopted, that will prevent them from interfering with each other's principles, objects, and arrangements. Shortly each member of all these societies will discover that they have but one and the same interest. These little matters, creating some temporary difference of feeling, being once adjusted, the rapidity of our progress will be much accelerated."

This was taken as a severe reflection upon the education society, and quite unnecessary to have been sent abroad in a newspaper any thing relating to a subject of private dealing; but as being not true, it was considered an injurious calumny calculated to mislead strangers, altogether, concerning the real state of the minds of these people in regard to that subject; to arrest which effect, it was thought eligible to answer and refute it in a manner equally public. Hereupon the society held a meeting and passed a resolve to depute Mr. Neef, one of their members, to draught a reply to be published in the Gazette. In consequence, Mr. Neef being requested in the name of the society, wrote such a reply as the following:—

"Mr. Editor—

"In your Gazette, of Nov. 29, you state that 'another cause of some dissatisfaction among the members of the education society arose from misconception among them as to the best line of separation between their lands and those of the other societies.' As this statement is so vague, indefinite, and incomprehensible, that out of a hundred readers of your paper, not one can derive any benefit from it, permit us to state what gave rise, not to our dissatisfaction but to our astonishment, a statement bottomed on incontrovertible facts known as such to every inhabitant of New-Harmony.

"When under the auspices of Mr. M'Clure the education society came into existence, a certain number of houses and proportion of land was thought necessary for their accommodation. Mr. Owen was then applied to for obtaining the above items; and after mature consideration a contract was made, with mutual consent, for those articles. The deed was signed by both parties and the bargain legally concluded. Some time back, and several months after the bargain had been struck, Mr. Owen wanted to have back some of the land.— This claim of Mr. Owen, and not our misconception of the lines, produced the dissatisfaction above mentioned.

"Again you say that 'they (meaning the members of the education society) thought some other line giving them more land in a particular direction inconvenient to their neighbors, was necessary for them.' Permit us to tell you that we thought no such thing. We thought, think yet, and shall go on thinking, that Mr. Owen ought to adhere to his contract and leave us in quiet possession of the land ceded to us.

"As to your prediction that a little reflection will convince us of this error, we hardly know what to make of it. We cannot conceive how either much or little reflection can convince us of having committed an error 'in coming to the determination of adhering to our contract.

"In behalf of the Education Society,
"J. NEEF."

This, after meeting the acceptance of the society, was presented to the editor with a request to publish it in the Gazette. He at first demurred, but agreed to do so (at least said he had no objection) if his name, being inserted in one clause as the surveyor who had run the lines of the land, should be stricken out: this was accordingly done, and the paper presented again; when, his father having caught it in his eye, peremtorily interdicted its insertion. He came to the writer protesting alarmingly against it, arguing that its publication could do no good, and it would overthrow the 'social system!' Upon which the writer interrogated him whether it were not all true; and he admitted it was true, but it would overthrow the system!! Thus was this reply refused a place in the Gazette. There might possibly be a trivial variation in phrase, and this very paper, of which the above is a literal transcript, was presented for publication, with Mr. Neef's signature and in his own hand, and the editor declined publishing it.

Now it is plain that this estate having been fairly conveyed to this society by a writing punctiliously drawn to the forms of law, as if by parties suspicious of each other, and not a cent of interest or principal being yet due, whether to Owen or M'Clure, neither of these men nor any of their deputies or assigns had any more right to take possession of the house No. 5, which was a part of the said estate so conveyed, and appropriate it to their own use or the use of any other person, aside of the behoof of this society, than either of them had to take possession of any house in Cincinnati, New-York, Quebec, or Edinburgh, belonging to any other individual or society whatever, and by force detain it in oppo-

11

sition to the will and interest of the proprietors. So
neither had Owen any right to re-enter upon or retake,
any of the land: nor had M'Clure any right to guarantee or abet him in retaking it. Yet this house, No. 5, was
occupied by a Madame Fratageot, keeping a school for
the inhabitants of No. 1, or south part of the town, in
opposition to that of the education society, of which
she had been expelled from membership for refusing to
teach such a number of children and of such ages as
the society appointed for her employ; she preferring to
take the whole of the teaching under her superintendence: it was occupied in part also by Mr. Owen, by
his son the editor of the Gazette, by M'Clure's brother,
in his absence, and by no person that was a member of
the society to which the house belonged. It became a
boarding school for young men of the other part of the
town; besides being the school of a multitude of young
children of both sexes, who resorted there every day.
Such things were hostile and injurious to the feelings of
the society, from the beginning; but they endured them.
Some have found reasons for believing that this same
female teacher was at the bottom of most of the overturning manœuvres of this place, as being willing by in-
gratiating herself with Owen and M'Clure, to promote
her own interest exclusive of others. In all their successive meetings the education society was unanimous
in protesting against yielding back any land to Owen;
they sent forward a memorial to M'Clure, then in New-
Orleans, claiming a defence of their soil; they, in effect,
forbade Owen to meddle with their land; still not being
of a litigious spirit, or willing to use violence. But
after all this, it seems that he, said Owen, was bent on
having the land, 'by hook or by crook,' as the saying is;
and, accordingly, in spite of the remonstrances of the
school society, in spite of their prohibition, in spite
of their unanimity to adhere to their contract, in the
teeth of the articles of the lease, in the teeth of the

law, and in the teeth of equity, did actually take, and
assume to his title, from 150 to 200 acres of the very
best of the land contained within their purchase, being
upland, dry, and well improved, and did sell or lease
a part of it, together with other property, to an individual or individuals, in a trade that took place afterwards, and of which we shall speak by and by.

Now, the education society had, for the sake of order,
passed a resolution that the privilege of using the Hall
for lectures, &c., should be obtained only by applying to
the meeting, or previously to any member, when a majority of the assembly might grant such privilege, the
keys being delivered, for keeping, to one Dr. Troost.—
On Sunday, the 14th of January, Mr. Owen having advertised the people of his intention to hold a lecture in
the Hall, yet having made no application to the society
for it, some persons burst the door open without paying
any regard to locks or keys, and he went in and dis-
coursed to the people.

It is easy to see that such a society as that of the education, which made nearer approaches to a republican
community than any others in the neighborhood, [the
members regularly assembling together, and, by a majority of the free and equal suffrages of male and female
members, making their own laws and regulations; whereas the people of No. 1, had no voice nor hand in their
government;] that such a society as this, bordering on
one that was under a despotic government, must infallibly cast a shade of indignity upon the other; and that
such as preferred despotism and monopoly, could readi-
ly be persuaded to embrace any expedients calculated
to dissolve and overthrow it. However it might be, it
so happened, that from some cause the members of this
education society dropped off one after another, and it
became very diminutive.

On Sunday, the 24th of January, Mr. Owen having
called an assembly of his *man*-machines, communicated

to them the intelligence of a GREAT SALE he had been making, or was about making, to an INDIVIDUAL, named, if I mistake not, Taylor, who came from the north part of Ohio; whereby the face of things should be changed, and a new community be formed; aye—a *commonwealth* owned by an individual! It came out that he actually sold to this individual, a man who professedly disregarded the 'system' of Mr. Owen, and openly declared he cared nothing about it, whom yet Mr. Owen in a private conversation afterwards, referring to his character and his capability of uniting the people in a community, pronounced to be WORTH MORE than any FIFTY MEN that had ever been in Harmony; that he actually sold off to this individual 1500 acres of land, a great part of which belonged to the estate of No. 1, according to all the former agreements which had been made or proposed, a part to what had been purchased by the school society, and some part beyond these limits; together with a flour mill, and some of the establishments in town, such as the tanyard, the tavern, the store, with all the cattle and the other personal property pertaining to his dominions. It was manifest at least that this Mr. Taylor took the immediate charge of things, having the whole managery of the cotton manufactory and the store.— This man immediately set up a distillery, and proceeded to manufacture strong drink.

The reader will have observed that the compact of a pretended community heretofore exhibited, was a very good implement for Owen, by which to get into his immediate possession the whole estate, as it previously lay under the incumbrance of leases and indentures, seeing that the compact gave the trustees the full and entire control of all the property, so that they could sell it any day, at wholesale or retail; and moreover, that there were to be conveyances of property from the members; which conveyances never were completed nor legally executed, and perhaps were never intended to be: for it has been rendered probable by Mr. Owen's saying the same day, that Taylor had written to him on the subject some considerable time ago, that negotiations existed for this private sale, prior to the formation of this compact, at least sooner than it could be carried into execution.

It was afterwards reported that, although the personal property was sold to Taylor, the real estate was only *leased* to him for a long time, except some particular buildings and trading establishments. Be this as it may, it was a substantial conveyance and rendition of the property to an individual's control.

February 1st was DOOMSDAY; the people having been forewarned in a meeting the preceding night, that a selection would be made [separation of the sheep from the goats] of such as were unfit to remain in the society and would be expelled, but were fit to form a community somewhere else, on Mr. Owen's lands; a proposal concerning which should meet them at the intendent's office the next night. In pursuance of which, in the course of the day about twenty heads of families received what some people call 'walking papers,' but which indeed were little other than billets of notice or invitation to meet agreeably to the token given out the night before. They assembled to receive their DOOM; which was, that they should settle on a half section of Mr. Owen's lands, on Mr. Owen's terms, on Mr. Owen's principles, according to Mr. Owen's plans, he advancing them some provisions for the first year; or, being allowed their rations one or two weeks longer, should thenceforth be independent of the society, and make the best of their way through the world by themselves. The rations, I think, held out about two weeks, for the reprobates; and two or three families agreed to accept of the offered land. Yet I understood that after those had removed their families and commenced clearing, the lease or indenture, which was left unfinished, coming to view, out of Mr. Owen's hands.

its conditions were so intolerable that they would not sign it. The rest prepared to quit the place, except some few that hired themselves to Taylor; and many took their leave of Harmony about this time.

While I lay sick three weeks, my scholars having all left me, Mr. Owen and his authorities, sans ceremonie, entered them at No. 5. On my recovery I had these replaced by a class of those who belonging to this household, of the boarding school, were of milder dispositions. and more easily manageable.

February 5th was DOGS' DOOMSDAY, or general dog killing; when all citizens of the canine brood were to be shot. Many were those that fell on that day.— But from whatever cause it was that they bore a peculiar fondness for this place, as we killed off the old, new ones seemed to come in, out of the country; so that we could scarce get rid of the society of this species.

This last manœuvre, of selling out the estate to an individual, swept away like a cobweb, the fairy dream of a common stock and a community.

A funeral was projected, of the ' *social system*,' and a coffin made and lettered; but such was the want of constancy and accord, even among the projectors, that, forasmuch as some person went into the armory and broke the coffin to pieces, in the night time preceding the appointed day of the procession which was to have performed the rites of sepulture, they abandoned their design. Thus the plan failed, for this time. It was well perhaps, however, for they had not given their subject the right name. They would better have named it the ' Owenian system,' or the ' Harmonian system.' But to call it the *social* system, did not seem to be right: for the true social system I take to be the system of commonwealths..

Thus has Mr. Owen gone on selling and buying, doing and undoing, taking and retaking, turning and overturning and re-overturning, bargaining, bantering, scheming, and manœuvring, and kept the whole town in a perpetual agitation, from the time he arrived from his voyage to England till this day. The whole course of his practice and preaching has had a bad effect upon the morals of the place. His practice tended to inspire cupidity, and his preaching tended to induce apathy or licentiousness. From the practice, all the inexperienced part of the population learned levity, duplicity, avarice, distrust, and partiality: and the preaching suggested to them that they need not be scrupulous about their conduct, for they were not blameable for their words or actions.— This pernicious doctrine, based on the rash position that 'man does not form his own character,' and on the absurd and catachrestical inference from it, that a person having such a persuasion or conviction cannot possibly blame another for any thing he does, had evidently a depraving influence upon the minds and hearts of people in all parts of the town. A general cupidity pervaded the place; individual wealth was venerated and worshipped. Moreover, the individual suffering, from the privations and embarrassments arising out of the continual shifting of arrangements, as well as undue circumscription of subsistence, deadened the wonted sympathy of many ingenuous souls. The sick could scarce get requisite attendance. Money was in higher repute than in any other town. Money, though for the most part an invisible being, became an object of worship. The sexes fought like cats about individual marriages. There was not true politeness between the single persons of the two sexes; but a dark, cold, sullen, suspicious temper, and a most intolerable miserly allusion to individual property as the standard of worth.— The single men of this town were generally obliged to make up their own beds for their lodgings, carry their clothes to the wash, call for and recover them when they could, as much as if they had belonged to an army.— Every one was *for himself*, as the saying is. No praise, no blame, no merit, no demerit, no right, no wrong, was a lesson that justified them in pursuing their individual gratification without regard to the feelings of others; and their education had taught them, that to command individual wealth, was their access to it. One woman, who had drunk deep at the current of this damnable doctrine, made declaration that if she were engaged to marry a *poor* man, and were standing up to pass the legal ceremony in confirmation of such contract, having that moment an opportunity to marry *another* man, who to her knowledge was possessed of six thousand dollars, she would immediately leave the first, and marry the last. An instance of so glaring dereliction of integrity and sense of moral obligation, was not every day seen or heard; but it may be supposed that the number was not small, comparatively, of those who were capable of it. In short, every thing has been propitious to infuse avarice, pride, selfishness, and every base principle and sentiment imaginable, into the female heart.

Here was no room for hospitality, generosity, charity, not even friendship, nor any of those gentle endearing social virtues which dignify while they embellish human nature. At their balls and social meetings, instead of learning affability, they learned little or nothing but pride.

The fact is, by the examples of this place and the appearances of intrigue, the morals of the people have been deteriorated during their residence in it: not that the bulk of those who were here last spring were not well calculated to be made good members of a commonwealth. Moreover, the greater part of the best of them have, one after another, disappeared. The fault is not in the dispositions the people brought with them, so much as in the management of the concerns of the place. It may be rationally presumed, and I should have no hesitation to pronounce, that not a single family or individual moved from any part of the country to *join* the community of New-Harmony, with a view to be idle and useless, and who did not *expect to labor* in *some* service, for the benefit of that community and for their own support, or who did not *cheerfully reckon* upon such service, as being *willing* to exert themselves usefully: though it is not denied that after their arrival, every discouragement was thrown in the way of the alacrity of such exertion. And it will be admitted also that there have generally been more or less of respectable gazing loungers loitering about the tavern, belonging to no society, but paying for their board with money; and perhaps some persons came and took their residence here who never *intended* to join a community or commonwealth at all.

The education society being dwindled to a small number, the remnant, whether from feeling a sense of their dependence on M'Clure's patronage, or an opinion that he was liable to be led about by those who felt interested in the disorganization of the society, adjourned their public meeting *sine die;* and the most of them began to think of seeking a resting place elsewhere. A plan was laid to make a settlement on the bank of the Ohio above Cincinnati. The granary or public eating-house, the cook-house, the meeting-house and sitting rooms, were left desolate, like a deserted citadel; and what were left of the society took their meals at the boarding school. Others from all parts of the town had their faces towards distant regions; and on Wednesday, the 21st day of March, (1827,) about eighty souls moving off in a body, made their exit, and entered a steamboat which was to ascend the Ohio.

On the 28th, the editor of the Gazette comes out with a smooth account of the affairs of New-Harmony, mentioning some of the effects of the changes, but not particularly pointing out their causes. He is candid enough, however, to acknowledge, or to profess an opinion, that Mr. Owen was in an error in the plan of changing the preliminary society into a community so soon. He says, paragraph 10th, that he [meaning Robert Owen] 'sought to abridge the period of human suffering by an immediate and decisive step, and the design was boldly conceived. Immediate success would have been a victory gained for the principles under every disadvantage, and as such, its effects would have been great and general.'

*Under every disadvantage!* aye; under the *special* disadvantage of an example of thrift, sharp trading, avaricious tenacity of individual wealth, book-keeping, close calculation of interest, loss and gain, interest upon interest, respect for the indications of high life and prosperity, tergiversation, and craft, set before them by their leader and teacher!——He says next, 'A failure would only afford proof that the conception, in this particular case, was not as practical as it was benevolent, inasmuch as the mass of the individuals collected at New-Harmony were not prepared for so advanced a measure.' I do not see even *this* proof. Why not as practical as benevolent? Where was the extraordinary benevolence in Mr. Owen's offering to sell a parcel of land and houses to a parcel of people for a hundred and thirty per cent. more than he gave for them? And yet this was the very proposed bargain, that they should give at least $140,000 for 2500 acres of land and the village of Harmony. Some one may start up and say, it was benevolent because he could have gained 300 per cent on his money in England. So then, if a man has a dozen watches which the probability is he *could have* sold in England for $50 a piece, and he chooses to come to America, and he sells them here for $20 a piece, it is benevolence; benevolence to the poor Americans that buy them! I say, no: there is no friendship nor benevolence in trade. There is no benevolence in selling goods or lands, nor in lending money on interest. What then was the decisive bold step by which Mr.

Owen sought to abridge the period of human suffering? Did he offer to GIVE land and houses to a parcel of poor people who subscribed to his doctrines, who were converts to his system, and who appeared to *him* to be so well prepared to enter into a perfect community? Did he offer to GIVE land and houses to these poor fellows who could not purchase it of their own government at a dollar and a quarter per acre. Did he offer to GIVE land and habitations to these poor people and convey it to them in perpetual trust without charge or expence, on condition of their making entire common property, and thence to let them be at ease and go on in the practice of the principles unincumbered and unobstructed with the anxiety of debt to individuals? NO! He offered to SELL it to them at a much higher price than land and comfortable habitations would have cost them, had they possessed the means to commence and insure a settlement on the national domains. He offered to let them have the estate for $140,000 with interest from the date of conveyance, and if any failure should happen, the whole estate might revert to Robert Owen and William M'Clure or their heirs. . This was the decisive adventurous step Mr. Owen took to cut short the period of human suffering. 'For so advanced a measure,' the people were not 'prepared.' The mass of the people were not altogether 'prepared' to bind themselves in an obligation of thousands to an individual, which they knew not how they should get wherewith to pay; and run the risk of making themselves slaves or tributaries or tenants at will. We have here been speaking of what took place in the spring of 1826; the very point of time to which the editor alludes when he speaks of an 'immediate and decisive step,' when the preliminary society was to be superseded by a community.

Further on, having spoken of the division into three societies, he says, 'Two of them then abandoned their separate independence, requesting Robert Owen with

the assistance of four trustees to take the general superintendence of their affairs, which were getting into some
confusion.' Now this was *not* first projected nor sought
by the people of these societies; they did not go and
request this of Robert Owen; the plan was first brought
forward and propounded by Robert Owen himself: and
it was acceded to only because of his offering to make
common stock of his estate and becoming a member:
this entered into the proposal, and this only made the
people accept of it. They were not well pleased with
the idea of an aristocratical form of government; and
the assurance of Mr. Owen's making common property
of his estate and himself becoming a member, was all
that reconciled them to it.

He proceeds—'The third society only, the 'education
society' under the auspices of William M'Clure, continued and still continues its original and separate form.'
So then, here is one society that outlives all the rest.
What is the reason? Is it not because it is independent
of Mr. Owen, in its organization, its government, and
the tenure of its estate. But even this is not permanent:
Why? Because it depends on an individual, William
M'Clure. No society is firmly founded that depends on
the will of an individual. But a commonwealth of free
men depending on the will of a wealthy individual for
its existence, is an absurdity. It is a palpable contradiction.

Under the auspices of William M'Clure! As if every
society must have some great tutelary patron upon
whom it depends, to sustain it and hold it together. We
speak of a very imperfect and infantile state of human
character when we speak of a *society* being dependent
on the patronage or under the auspices of an *individual*,
who is separate from it.——After speaking of the society
under the trustees, or No. 1, being broken up because it
did not pay its expences, he says—'A remedy presented
itself in the voluntary association, out of the population

of New-Harmony, of those individuals who had mutual confidence in one another's intentions and mutual pleasure in one another's society. Land and assistance for the first year were offered to those who chose to unite in this way; and the consequence was the formation of another community on the Harmony lands.' Now this 'voluntary association' means precisely that of the few families among those who had received their 'walking papers' after the sale and conveying away of the estate to individuals, who accepted of the offer of wild lands, not being able to settle elsewhere at a distance. They had their doom; they had their alternative. By stress of circumstances they were impelled, as it were, to unite upon an expedient that offered itself, for subsistence. If the truth is to be known, they were not the most concordant in their feelings and views, of all people that ever associated together: they adventured to settle, with their families, on Mr. Owen's lands, not because they would have preferred it to any other place had they possessed means to purchase some more desirable situation wholly independent of him; but because they could not command those means. This was the 'voluntary association' of persons 'having mutual confidence,' &c. There might be two or three that associated, that were *not* of the number of those who had received walking papers, or been the subjects of a selection: but the sale and individualizing of the property was the forerunner and cause of all this associating. The society was breaking up; the pretended common stock was sold out, in part at least, and the estate peculiarized to individual control. Hence different recourses were embraced to obtain a subsistence where things were less fluctuating, and where they might enjoy rational liberty. The statement is very illusive; for whereas it says 'voluntary association, out of the population of New-Harmony, of those individuals,' &c.—not a soul of those who associated to take wild lands, went from any other part of the town but that which was called No. 1: every one of those people were of those who had lived in that society, under the trustees. Yet the school society was a part of the population of New-Harmony; and there were persons in this, who had as much 'mutual confidence' as any of those. The statement would have been more ingenuous and more in accord with facts, if it had said 'association out of the population of No. 1, particularly out of those who had received their warning that they must leave the society at all events.'

In the Gazette of the 4th of April, the editor puts out a studied and plausible apology, for not publishing a certain piece which he calls a ' vindication of the character of one of his fellow citizens.' This piece proved, upon inquiry, to be the following one from the pen of Dr. Troost, who having about seventeen years' acquaintance with Mr. Neef, and with Mr. Jackson a former pupil of said Neef, found it his duty to say something in favor of the latter, as in the capacity of a teacher, that is, as a man having a particular faculty of *teaching* by a method which had been found to be of extensive and lasting utility in its effects, in opposition to the prejudices of some who had but a short and superficial acquaintance with the man.

### (" *For the New-Harmony Gazette.*)

" When we hear unmerited praise, we ought to think it can do no harm; it may take in some gull or other, but it is generally of a short duration. But when we see innocence persecuted, when we see malice, ignorance, and fanaticism employ their craft to destroy the character of a man of merit, then it is the duty of him who is above the machinations of the envious, to counteract it as much as in his power. The latter sentiment is applicable upon Joseph Neef. His unprejudiced mind and enlightened mode of teaching, have given him many enemies. The

fitst has armed against him fanaticism; the second, ignorance and envy. I have been for seventeen years
acquainted with J. Neef: I have found that every one
whose mind was not blinded by fanaticism, who was not
envious of the real merit which he possessed, was the
friend of Neef.—As for the manner of education, all
those whom I know of his pupils have done well afterwards. Some of them are the ornaments of the rank in
which they have been placed, and the whole are more
enlightened and unprejudiced than the generality of men.

"Accident put, a few days ago, in my hand, a new
publication, being 'a new method of teaching languages,'
written by Doctor Samuel Jackson, one of the pupils of
Joseph Neef. I have known Dr. Jackson these sixteen
years; his conduct has been such that he has gained the
esteem of his fellow citizens in general. No one was
more active, even at the risk of his own life, than he in
aiding the sufferers during the last yellow fever in Philadelphia; far more than his professional duty required.—
He lectured on materia medica in the apothecaries' college with applause.—The seeds of this conduct were
sown during his education by J. Neef. See here the
passage of the abovementioned book, in which Dr. J.
confesses this himself: 'But here we must stop short to
pay a willing and grateful tribute of veneration to the
great and enlightened mind of Joseph Neef, the author
of a work on education, Philadelphia, 1808. We had
the advantage of learning French under this gentleman,
and of acquiring at the same time many excellent precepts in the art of teaching. Whither he is gone we
know not, nor have we been able to ascertain; but could
these pages reach him, his great soul would not revolt
at even this humble attempt to apply those principles
which it was his design to infuse into the whole system
of education. Hail thou generous friend of my youth,
and the friend of all mankind! *Te socium studeo, scri-
bendes reversibus esse.*'          "G. TROOST."

But the editor of the Gazette was so scrupulous about admittting into it any 'discussion of private character' whatever, that he rejected this communication; not recollecting perhaps that in the seventeenth number of the first volume of this same Gazette, [when Mr. Jennings was editor, but when the proprietors and conductors of the paper were, if ever, under an impressive sense of their duty to conform to the principles of its prospectus, so recently displayed to the world,] a considerable long string of syllogistical preaching was drawn into its columns, to prove logically that Mr. Robert Owen was wiser than his cotemporaries, as a political economist.

The greatest part of the town was now resolved into individual lots; a grocery was established opposite the tavern; painted sign boards begun to be stuck up on the buildings, pointing out places of manufacture and trade; a sort of wax figure and puppet show was opened at one of the boarding houses, charging twenty-five cents for adults and twelve and a half for children; and every thing went on in the old style.

On the 20th of April, William M'Clure returned from his sojourn at New-Orleans; and more people were preparing to depart from the education society to ascend the Ohio.

*New-Harmony, April 22, 1827.*

# FIVE WEEKS MORE.

AFTER Wm. M'Clure's return, it seems there was much bantering of Mr. Owen with him, and many bargains made, from which the latter immediately after their completion, always, as the saying is, *flew.* On the 30th of April, was posted on the walls of some buildings the following advertisement:

"Notice is hereby given to all whom it may concern, forewarning them not to trust Robert Owen on my account, as I am determined not to pay any debts of his, or in any way be responsible for any transaction he may have done or may attempt to do in my name.

"WM. M'CLURE.
"New-Harmony, April 30, 1827."

Immediately under this, in a short time afterwards appeared the following:

"Having just now seen a very extraordinary advertisement put upon some of the houses in this place and signed Wm. M'Clure, it becomes necessary in my own defence to inform the public that the partnership between Wm. M'Clure and myself is in full force, and that I shall pay any contract made either by Wm. M'Clure or myself on the partnership account.

"ROB'T. OWEN.
"New-Harmony, 30th April, 1827."

I spyed both on the wall of the education society's brick storehouse at eventide: the next day none were to be seen. In the course of this next day, (being May 1st,) Wm. M'Clure prosecuted Robert Owen for 40,000 dollars, about the amount he had paid him, or of some bonds he had got of Rapp, with a view to make him give him a deed in fee simple, of the estate he had bought of him, or refund him such amount of money. Whatever particular view it was he had, it seems the deed was his primary object. Owen was arrested by the sheriff, but was taken off by some friends, by a promise to deliver him up at a certain hour if a settlement should not intervene. The hour elapsed, and thenceforward he was not found in the reach of the sheriff, being shut up in his room. Meanwhile it seems he had despatched his son William to Mount Vernon, to get out a writ against M'Clure for a demand of 90,000 dollars. This writ was obtained. But the next day, some persons interposing, an arrangement was brought about, by which Owen gave to M'Clure, the deed in fee simple, which he wished, and they proceeded to settle all their affairs. It was supposed that, upon the whole matter, M'Clure owed nothing to Owen: it seems there was some crookedness in the book accounts on the part of Mr. Owen; it being said he had made a charge of forty dollars for books used by the school; and the school never had had any of him. However, in a few days all their matters were somehow settled.

On Sunday, the 6th day of May, Mr. Owen having, by way of written notification, advertised all the *man*-machines in Harmony and the neighboring societies, that a general meeting would be held, gave a discourse or address to an assembly in the Hall; which was thought to be a sort of farewell, he having been making preparations to go to Europe.—The address was as follows:—

# ADDRESS

*Delivered by* Robert Owen, *on Sunday, the 6th of May, 1827, in the New-Harmony Hall, to the Citizens of New-Harmony, and to the Members of the neighboring Communities.*

A second year has just expired since the experiment was commenced in this place to supersede the individu-

al by the co-operative system of union and equality under the form of a preliminary society.

It is known to you, that the persons who composed
this society were entire strangers to each other; that
some had come from every state in the Union, and some
from almost every kingdom in Europe:

That the society was instituted to enable these persons to become acquainted with each other, so that those
who were capable of acting faithfully and cordially together might afterwards form a community upon the social system:

That, after the preliminary society was constituted,
and the members had elected a committee to govern
themselves, I went to Europe, and returned again in
about nine months:

That, soon after my return, it was proposed, that a
community of common property and equality should be
formed from among the members of the preliminary society; and many of you know that it was my intention
that the community should at first consist of those only,
who had acquired confidence in each other's qualifications for such a state of society. It is also known to
many who are present, that this intention was frustrated
by a motion being made at one of the public meetings,
that *all* the members of the preliminary society should
be admitted members of the community; and this motion
was too popular to be resisted by those who did not
otherwise expect to become members. From that period, the most intelligent among the population foresaw
that this measure would retard the formation of one
large united community in the town of Harmony: there
were too many opposing habits and feelings to permit
such a mass, without more instruction in the system, to
act at once cordially together.

This singularly constituted mass, however, contained
materials, out of which, by patience and perseverance,
several communities might be ultimately formed; and

all my subsequent measures were directed to accomplish this object.

Although many who were here at that time were unprepared to be members of a community of common property and equality, yet there was much good feeling among the population generally; and, if the schools had been in full operation, upon the very superior plan which I had been led to expect, so as to convince the parents by ocular demonstration of the benefits which their children would immediately derive from the system, it would have been, I think, practicable, even with such materials, with the patience and perseverance which would have been applied to the object, to have succeeded in amalgamating the whole into a community.

You also know, that the chief difficulty at this time arose from the difference of opinion among the professors and teachers brought here by Mr. M'Clure, relative to the education of the children, and to the consequent delay in putting any one of their systems into practice.

Having been led to entertain very high expectations of the abilities of these individuals, I looked to them to establish very superior arrangements for the instruction of all ages, and I was induced to suppose, that the population would be compensated for the delay in the execution, by the unequalled excellence of the system when put into practice. But, in consequence of the unlimited confidence which I placed in these individuals to execute this the most important part of my plan, in a very superior manner, you all know how much I have been disappointed. Instead of forming one well-digested arrangement, in which all the children should have the benefit of the superior qualifications possessed by each professor and instructor, each principal teacher undertook the entire instruction of a certain number of pupils, by which arrangement they were prevented from associating with the other pupils.

By this error in their practice, the object, which I

had the most at heart, could not be attained: the children were educated in different habits, dispositions and feelings,—when it was my most earnest desire, that *all* the children should be educated in similar habits and dispositions, and be brought up truly as members of one large family, without a single discordant feeling.

It is true, each of the professors and principal teachers possessed considerable abilities and acquirements in particular branches of education; but the union of the best qualities and qualifications of several of even the best modern teachers is required to form the character of the rising generation, as it ought to be formed, to enable children, when they attain maturity, to become sufficiently rational and intelligent to be good and useful members of the social system.

As these difficulties regarding the education of our children were to be overcome, as well as many others to which these gave rise, I waited patiently for such changes of circumstances as would enable me to make a progress towards my object. With deep interest I attended to the various changes which the different parties desired to make, and I always met their wishes, as far as circumstances would admit. I did so, because I had not yet attained sufficient knowledge of the persons or localities of the country to act with my customary decision.

These changes gave me a more speedy insight into the character of the population, and enabled me to obtain a better knowledge of those, who were in some degree prepared to commence the social system. They also elicited a knowledge of the means by which future communities might be the most easily and safely formed; and to me this was invaluable experience, to be hereafter applied for the benefit of the inhabitants of this country, and of Great Britain, where the productive classes are now so much in want of some effective change of system for their relief.

Among those who first came here, there were many with whom none could be found to unite in community: these persons became a great obstacle to the progress of our proceedings. It was necessary for the safety, comfort and happiness of those who remained, and for the success of the system itself, that they should remove.

The difficulty arose from the expense of their removal, and from the necessity of informing them, that they were not such members as would be admitted into communities at their commencement. If I paid for the removal of one family, all would expect to be assisted in like manner,—an expenditure my funds would not admit of, after the large sums which had been previously invested in the experiment; and no one would like to be informed, that none could be found who would agree to admit them to become members of their community. This, however, was a difficulty which it was absolutely necessary, for the sake of all, should be overcome.

That every one might have a fair and equal chance, I proposed to supply land, in proportion to numbers, on the estate of New-Harmony, to all who would associate, even in small numbers, to commence a community, and that they should have aid in food and implements of husbandry, to the extent that our means would afford. This was a public offer, made equally to all, and those who came here with the view of forming communities accepted it, and are now industriously occupied in preparing crops for this season.

Those persons who would not, or could not so connect themselves, were informed, that they must leave Harmony, or support themselves by their own industry, until they could find persons of a good character, who would join them in forming a community.

This measure, unpleasant as it was to my feelings, became unavoidable, to prevent the entire loss of the property which had been appropriated to carry on the experiment; and by this course of proceeding those persons who were in a condition to promote the social system, were relieved from the permanent support of those individuals, who were daily diminishing the fund which had been devoted for a more general, beneficial purpose.

Under these circumstances many families, as you know, left New-Harmony, with their feelings more or less hurt,—and, in proportion to the knowledge of, and love for the principles, really possessed by each of them, are, no doubt, their statements for or against my proceedings, and for or against the social system.

This period, the most unpleasant and trying to my feelings of any which I have had to pass through,—for my object in coming here was to benefit all, and, if possible, to injure none,—has happily passed. The social system is now firmly established; its principles are daily becoming better understood; the natural and easy means of forming communities have been developed by our past experience. Already eight independent communities of common property and equality, have been formed upon the New-Harmony estate, exclusive of Mr. M'Clure's, or the education society, and of the town of New-Harmony, which has naturally become the place for the reception of strangers, who have a desire to join some of the existing communities, or to form others.

New-Harmony is therefore now literally surrounded by independent communities, and applications are made almost daily, by persons who come from far and near, to be permitted to establish themselves in a similar manner. The essential difference between our first and the present proceedings is this: At the commencement, strangers to each other's character, principles, habits, views, and sentiments, were associated together, to acquire a knowledge of each other and to learn the practice of the social system: but now, those only asso-ciate in communities who were previously well acquainted with each other, who possess similar habits, sentiments and feelings, and who have made some advance in obtaining knowledge of the principles and practices requisite to be known by those, who become members of communities of equality and common property. Experience has proved, that between these two modes of proceeding the difference is great indeed!

Since those persons have removed from New-Harmony, who, from one cause or another, were disposed to leave us, the remainder of the population are, you perceive, gradually taking those situations, best suited to their inclinations and former habits, and in some instances, the occupations have formed among themselves a kind of preparatory society, and are doing well. The lands of the communities around us, have been put in a good state of cultivation, and are well fenced; there is, as you see, at this time, every appearance of abundance of fruit and of all kinds of food, and materials for clothing, and no want of industry to preserve the former and to manufacture the latter. Upwards of thirty good cabins have been lately finished, upon the lands of communities Nos. 2, 3, and 4, and yet not a spare room can be obtained for any who may come to us.

The town and immediate vicinity of New-Harmony, you perceive, have been greatly improved lately, and other important improvements are in progress. No scite for a number of communities in close union together can be finer than that which surrounds us; its natural situation and the variety of its productions exceed every thing of the kind I have ever seen in Europe or America. The rich land, intermixed with islands, woods, rivers and hills in a beautiful proportion to each other, presents, from our high grounds, a prospect which highly gratifies every intelligent stranger. It is true, misconceptions of our proceedings and of our present state are gone forth, to the great grief of those, who were looking with intense interest, to an amelioration of the

condition of all classes of society, from the measures
which were to commence here; but these reports have
been most beneficial; they have prevented us from being
quite overwhelmed with numbers, and they have also
obtained for us time to organize the new arrangement
of employments, and to promote the formation of new
communities.

These operations have been going forward so successfully, that perhaps no pleasure has been more pure
than that, which I have enjoyed for some time past, in
my daily visits to some one of these new establishments,
where by the industry of the persons engaged, I saw the
sure foundation laid, of independence for themselves
and for their children's children, through many generations; from the new order of things arising around
them, they must become a superior race of intelligent,
virtuous, and happy beings, whose chief occupation,
after a few years of temperance and industry, will be
to distribute to others, the means of becoming as independent, useful and happy as themselves.

I had also made my arrangements, to settle before
my departure for Europe, every outstanding account
against myself and those concerned with me in this
establishment and experiment, that no obstacle should
remain, after my departure, to impede the progress
and success of the young colonies; and looking back
through the two years just expired, I could not but feel
an almost inexpressible delight, an inward satisfaction
from reflecting upon the obstacles which had been overcome, and from viewing, in the mind's eye, the cheering
prospects which are before us. The latter, although
not exactly in the way I expected, far exceed the most
sanguine anticipations I formed at the commencement
of the experiment here, and induce a belief that nothing can prevent the rapid spread of the social system
over the United States.

While preparing for my journey to Europe, and just

as I was going to set out, an event occurred, as you know, which arose, as I must believe, from some extraordinary misconception in the minds of some of our well meaning friends, which fortunately has detained me some days longer among you. These misconceptions are, I believe, now completely removed, and I have had, by this delay, the pleasure .of receiving and of becoming acquainted with some highly respectable families from the south, who have travelled several hundred miles, on purpose to live some time among you, and to make themselves familiar with the new system. I trust you will be kind to them and to each other. I intend to take my departure in a few days, and I have now only to wish you success in your glorious undertaking and to bid you farewell.

ROBERT OWEN.

Immediately after the close of this address, he was contradicted, particularly by one of the audience, as to several of the assertions he had made therein, in a manner that very much baffled his vindication, and, as it were, put him to a stand. The address was published in the Gazette of the following Wednesday, but not a word of the opposition it met.

On the 11th or 12th of May, one of the M'Clures sent to Mr. Joseph Neef a request that he would write an answer to the foregoing address of Mr. Owen: whereupon he, said Neef, sat down and wrote as followeth:

### A LETTER TO ROBERT OWEN,
#### CONCERNING HIS VALEDICTORY ADDRESS.

Sir—

In your valedictory address of the 6th of May, you attempt to account for the failure you experienced in establishing at this place a community of equality and common property. This failure, being an effect, must have a cause. You assign two causes; but neither of them is the true one. It is neither the superabundance of the 'opposing habits and feelings of the mass of individuals collected at Hew-Harmony, nor the undertaking of each principal teacher of the entire instruction of a certain number of pupils,' to which we must look for the true cause of the miscarriage of your scheme. Your conduct, Sir, is the sole and only source of this abortion; and of this fact I am going to convince you against your will, if you take the trouble to read this address of mine.

All the individuals who came to New-Harmony, had two objects in view. The first was to get rid of the inconveniences and miseries of the individual system; and the second, with those that had children, to have their children properly educated. Now, Sir, you have done every thing in your power to thwart these two objects. Hence your failure.

All your multifarious writings, speeches, lectures, addresses, teem with denunciations against individual property, against competition, against inequality. Common property, co-operation, equality, form, according to your doctrine, the true and only basis of social happiness. Every man that has but one grain of common sense, must perceive that you are right, that your doctrine coincides with the lessons of experience: and had your practice and conduct been in concord with your professions, the social system, by this time, would be as solidly fixed at this place as the rock———*que mola sua stat.*

But it seems that all the various preachers are doomed to be alike in one respect, namely, in making their doctrines disagree with their practice.

I arrived here on the 20th of March, 1826, and the first thing that struck me with astonishment and dismay was to hear of nothing but valuation of houses, barns, stables, land; of making bargains and contracts, of 'buying cheap and selling dear,' of capital and its interest; so that, having tried to escape out of the 'frying-pan' I felt myself plunged into a red hot furnace!

The first thing that you attempted after my arrival was to saddle us with a debt of $160,000 and an annual interest of $8000.

Now, eleven years' experience in this western country had fully convinced me that, without discovering a gold mine on this New-Harmony estate, it would be impossible to discharge such a debt or to pay its annual interest. I proposed, therefore, that either you should make us a present of these 2,500 acres of land, or be contented with the very equitable sum of $4 per acre, that is to say, $10,000, which between about one hundred individuals, would have amounted to $100 a head. This sum we could have raised among ourselves and thus become the owners of the land without any incumbrance. This was the only way in which a genuine commonwealth could be formed here. To talk of common property, co-operation, of industry, economy, carefulness, &c. &c. as you did, to a set of people that did not own an inch of the ground on which they lived, that were liable to be expelled every moment, that had no interest in being either frugal, industrious, economical or careful, was just as wise as if one of our southern planters should preach such doctrines to his community of black citizens. To make any set of human beings industrious, careful, &c. &c. you must make it their palpable interest to be so. But what interest had the people here to be industrious? Just as much as the negroes in any of our black communities, called cotton or sugar plantations.

Had you followed my earnest advice, and made this place our real and permanent home, by giving, or selling it to us at the reasonable price I proposed, an excellent commonwealth would have been established in the twinkling of an eye. Never were there better materials collected for such a purpose.

But unluckily you took it into your head to establish
a kind of feudal barony [for I can find no softer term to
designate your establishment,] and as of all men we
backwoods people are the least proper to live in such a
state of society, all those that could, in any way, find
the means to escape from such a state of things, necessarily availed themselves of their power of locomotion.
You boast of the number of *communities* that have
sprung up on your estate.   The editor of your Gazette
denominated these establishments *colonies*; and I think
this latter name more appropriate than the term you
employ.   For what is a community?   Certainly a state
of society in which every thing belongs to the people
forming the society.   But in your communities the land
and houses unquestionably belong to you alone.   The
improvements made by your tenants increase the value
of your estate.   Their labour and industry contribute
to enhance the value of your individual property. Such
a misnomer deserves but a transient smile, and therefore
I shall say no more about it.

Let us now examine some of your assertions made in
your valedictory address.   You say, that 'after your return from Europe it was your intention that the community should at first consist of those only who had
acquired confidence in each other's qualifications for
such a state of society,' which means, that the society
should consist only of such simpletons as would suffer
themselves to be saddled with an enormous debt and its
annual interest; a debt and interest which it was
morally and physically impossible ever to discharge.
You speak of confidence: but, pray, how was it possible that any of your proselytes should have any confidence in one another, when your conduct, so diametri-
cally opposed to your professions, your evasive an-
swers, your tergiversations, your perpetual changes of
measures, had necessarily annihiliated every vestige of
confidence in the founder of the system?   There was

not a man here who could see half an inch before his nose, who was not fully convinced that your scheme was nothing but what in this country we term a speculation. But you have made vast sacrifices, sustained immense pecuniary losses. Very true; but this has been the fate of many other speculators.

"This singularly constituted mass contained materials out of which by patience and perseverance several communities might be ultimately formed; and all my subsequent measures were directed to accomplish this object."

Permit me to tell you that you have a singularly unlucky knack at telling a story. I am sure that the best guesser in New-England will never be able to hit upon the true meaning of your above quoted sentence, unless assisted by my interpretation. When you began to perceive the truth of the assertion that it would be impossible to discharge the enormous debt of $160,000 and its annual interest of $8000, you concluded that it would be safer to parcel out the load between several masses of individuals. Hence the separate bargains with the education, pastoral, agricultural, mechanic, societies. This is the true statement of the matter: it does not run quite so smooth as your sentence; but its intelligibility will make up for its deficiency in smoothness.

"Although many who were here at that time [after your return from Europe] were unprepared to be members of a community of common property and equality; yet there was much good feeling among the population generally; and if the schools had been in full operation upon the very superior plan which I had been led to expect, so as to convince the parents by ocular demonstration of the benefits which their children would immediately derive from the system, it would have been, I think, practicable even with such materials, with the patience and perseverance which would have been applied to the object, to *have succeeded* in amalgamating the whole into a community."

'It would have been practicable to have succeeded' is not English. It would have been practicable to *succeed.* This is the way in which plain Englishmen express themselves. This, however, is mending the matter grammatically only, without making sense of your expression. For practical success, is, with your permission, nonsense. The amalgamation of some heterogeneous substances may be practicable. But no man of sense, who understands what he says or writes, will talk of the practicability of the success of amalgamating them. To make, therefore, both grammar and sense of your phrase, you must in your next edition, say that it would have been practicable to amalgamate, &c.

But to proceed to more serious considerations—what do you mean with your 'even with such materials?' As the words stand, every man must conclude that the people congregated at New-Harmony were the most worthless set of animals ever jumbled together on any given spot. 'Even with such materials' means even with such a set of worthless dogs. You assign no other reason for the bad opinion you entertain of the character of the New-Harmony population, but their opposing habits and feelings. Opposing habits and feelings prove nothing either for the goodness or badness of character; and therefore your assertion of the worthlessness of your materials has no other foundation but your assertion. Though I am sure that my bare assertion would far outweigh yours with any man that knows any thing about you and me, yet I will not confine myself to naked asseverations. I assert, therefore, that the materials collected at New-Harmony were the very best for forming an excellent community, for the following *reasons.* The married people came here to have their children well educated: and all of them were eager to escape from the miseries of individual society. These two positions are absolutely undeniable. Now people that had sense enough to perceive that a community of co-operation.

of common property, would be the best and perhaps the only means to secure these objects, were, without a shadow of doubt, the very best materials to form such a community. You say that 'many who were here at that time were unprepared to be members of a community of common property and equality,' and I assert that you were the only man averse to such a state of things. In spite of your altisonant professions with which I was acquainted long before I arrived at this place, I never expected that you would part with your pelf and contribute by your labor to the production of the necessaries and comforts of life which you enjoy. Experience, my only teacher, has taught me that monied men cling with as much tenacity to their money as a remora to a ship.

You think that had the schools been properly organized and carried on, it would have been possible to organize a community; [for this is the amount of your long winded phrase.] I wish you would imitate the editor of your Gazette, and exchange the word *community* for the word *colony.* But this *en passant.* You ought to say that a proper organization of the schools would have induced many parents to stay at New-Harmony; a proof of the excellent character of our population, who, disappointed in a material point of their expectations, would nevertheless have consented to remain in a kind of bondage, solely to promote the welfare of their offspring. As your words stand, your readers will be induced to believe that none of the scholastic establishments was organized and put in operation. This however is notoriously untrue. Every inhabitant of New-Harmony knows that I lost not a moment to organize my department. I had to procure benches and tables for the school rooms, beds and bedsteads for the sleeping rooms, tables and benches for the eating room; forks, knives, plates, cups, in short every article absolutely indispensable for the accommodaion of 170 chil-

dren, the number allotted to my superintendence.—
Under every possible disadvantage, which I shall not
mention, and which every inhabitant of this place is acquainted with, I began my operations. My unremitted
exertions triumphed over every obstacle, and in two
short months, order, regularity, and harmony, were established. My children were well classed, their rough
edges were wearing off; my teachers began to under-
stand the rationale of my operations; a mutual attach-
ment between the instructors and their pupils was established; when you, in an evil hour, became the willing
tool of a certain person that shall be nameless, for des-
troying my school.

But let us see some more of your positions.

"The chief difficulty, at this time, arose from the difference of opinion among the professors and teachers
brought here by Mr. M'Clure, relative to the education
of the children; and to the consequent delay in putting
any one of their systems into practice."

This sentence of yours is absolutely unintelligible.—
'The chief difficulty' in doing what? in establishing
communities, or in organizing the schools? What had
the alleged difference of opinion to do in the establishment of communities? Did it prevent me from establishing my school? Certainly not. What, in the name
of wonder, do you then mean with your chief difficulty?

"The children were educated in different habits, dispositions, and feelings." Just three paragraphs before
this, you say that if the schools had been in full operation, &c.; which in plain English means that the schools
were not in operation, that the children of course were
not educated: and here you assert that the children were
educated in different habits, dispositions, and feelings.
By what law of dialectics you will reconcile these two
assertions I do not know; and as I do not perceive any
means to effect an agreement between them, I shall,
without ceremony, leave them to their fate.

"It was my earnest desire, that all the children should be educated in similar habits and dispositions, and brought up truly as members of one large family, without a single discordant feeling."

I do not know whether this was your most earnest desire or not; but I positively know that it was mine.— You cannot but recollect, what I told you and Mr. M'Clure concerning this very subject, when the establishing of an independent school society was in agitation. I told you that if you adopted such a disjointing scheme, we should never have any school at this place; for this simple reason, that the parents could not afford to pay individually for the education, food, and clothing, of their children. And this prediction of mine was verified soon enough. Had your desire been in unison with mine, you would have listened to my plain reasonings, and never have consented to the establishment of such a state of things.

"The union of the best qualities and qualifications of several of even the best modern teachers is required, to form the character of the rising generation, as it ought to be formed, to enable children when they attain maturity to become sufficiently rational and intelligent to be good and useful members of the social system."

Very fine, indeed; but not very definite. As you know so much about the matter, what does your *several* mean? Half a dozen, a dozen, or how many? Please to specify the number of teachers requisite to transform a child into a rational and intelligent being. As the matter is all-important, the vagueness of your number cannot be satisfactory. But is it really such a terrible affair to transmute a child into a rational and intelligent being? Let us see. And first, what is a rational and intelligent being? A rational man is a man who consults experience and acts in conformity with the results of his expeence; whose actions are invariably based on his knowledge and not on his belief. An intelligent man is a man who knows how to trace effects to their causes, who knows how to discriminate between what is conducive to his welfare, and what has a tendency to injure him. And do you think it such a mighty affair to form such a man? Nothing easier in the world. Train a number of boys to gather knowledge by their own senses, to consult experience in every instance, to analyze, to examine, to investigate every thing, to believe nothing. Convince them by their daily experience that the more they trust and believe, the more they are liable to be cheated and imposed upon; the less they believe, the less they will be gulled; and if they believe nothing they will never be deceived; and you will produce men as rational and intelligent as you may wish them to be. Now I contend that this task may be performed by one single individual, your pompous sentence notwithstanding.

"With deep interest I attended to the various changes which the different parties [teachers] desired to make."

Permit me to tell you that I never dreampt of making any changes, and consequently I request you to segregate me henceforth from this change-desirous society.

"I always met *their* wishes as far as circumstances would admit."

I am very sorry that you cannot utter one truth without alloy. If you had said that you complied with the wishes of the above stated anonymous person, you would have told the whole truth and nothing but the truth, as every really conscientious man ought to do.

"I did so, because I had not yet attained sufficient knowledge of the persons or localities of the country to act with my customary decision."

Such language as this savours too much the nabob to be relished by the backwoodsmen. It may be well enough for the cotton-spinning paupers of Great Britain; but our American stomachs cannot digest such stuff.— As to your knowledge of this country, I am fully convinced, without your confession, that it is below zero; and

I am afraid that you will never acquire a sufficient stock to be of any service to you.

"My object in coming here was to benefit all, and if possible to injure none."

If this has been your mark in coming here, then let me inform you that there never was a more unskilful archer than you.

To be candid, however, for one benefit we are certainly indebted to you; and this benefit consists in knowing that to trust and believe is a sure way of being imposed upon.

I have neither time nor inclination to make any further remarks on the contents of your valedictory address; and I beg you to believe that those I thought proper to make, did not originate in any spirit of enmity to you.—I never in my life knowingly and willingly injured any body. What I wrote I know to be literally true; and every man or woman that is conversant with the transactions of this place, will without hesitation acknowledge every word to be the unvarnished truth. As to the manner of expressing my sentiments, I confess it to be rather uncourtly. But this is the common fault of this country of freedom. I verily believe that a twenty-one years' residence in such a country would transform the greatest sycophant into an intrepid truth-teller. Judge, then, what effect such a length of time must have produced on me, who, by the bye, never was very well qualified for a courtier. Fare thee well.

JOSEPH NEEF.

*New-Harmony, May* 13, 1827.


Mr. Owen had given out word that he intended to return to New-Harmony in December next. Nevertheless, he did not start off immediately after his farewell, and conformably to his alleged preparation; but remained in the place several weeks longer.

Mr. Phiquepal, the teacher, was, by order of Mr.

M'Clure, excluded from the church, where his pupils learned trades, and likewise from the brick building, which with great labor he had made a very commodious kitchen and eating house for all his scholars and his assistants, the whole of which building was again to be converted to a blacksmith's shop. He thence retreated to a room in the house No. 1, in which by sufferance of Mr. Owen and his agents he kept his school. In short, the education society dwindled to nothing; none were to remain but those who should be employed on hire; Mr. M'Clure having sustained losses, began to be somewhat more circumscriptive in his allowances of sustenance to the remnant that, lingering in suspense, hung to a slender thread of the broken union; and the face of the whole town began to wear more and more the appearance of three distinct lordships.

I continued teaching in the boarding school till the 2d day of June, when myself and fifteen other persons took leave of Harmony, to ascend the Ohio from Mount Vernon. The same day two other Harmonian gentlemen came out, in order to descend the river, for Missouri; and stood waiting for a boat as we left the shore of Mount Vernon. We arrived safe at Cincinnati on the evening of the 6th: the very place where I now sit writing in the latter part of July, 1827.

Mr. Owen tarried at New-Harmony about four weeks after the time of his bidding farewell to the *man*-machines, and, reaching Cincinnati six hours before my arrival, stopped in this place two or three days, then pursued his travels towards the Atlantic shore, in order to embark for England.

Although the greatest part of Mr. Owen's address of the 6th of May, was very ably refuted by Mr. Neef; yet, several passages remaining which claimed attention and were proper objects of criticism, I myself wrote a reply to these, [while at New-Harmony,] reviving the subject where he had dropped it; which reply, since those newspapers that have the most extensive circulation, are not very easy to admit pieces of such length, unless they happen to be about an *election* of Tom, Dick, or Harry, to one sort of office or another, or about some *public dinner* given to some public jack-ass, I have taken into my head to tack, just here, to the conclusion of my Harmony journal, like a wheelbarrow tied to the hind end of a loaded waggon.

## COPY OF A LETTER TO ROBERT OWEN, ESQ.

*IN REPLY TO SOME PASSAGES IN HIS VALEDICTORY ADDRESS AT NEW-HARMONY.*

SIR—

In your farewell discourse, of the 6th of May, addressed to those among the remnant of the inhabitants of this place who listened to you, and through them to the world by means of your Gazette, you labor ingeniously to varnish over your proceedings here and to mislead the public mind with regard to the motives and effects of what has been transacted in the place. The address was prepared to be sent abroad, and it was evidently calculated with design to illude strangers at a distance who never saw New-Harmony, especially those who never *will* see it, in order to keep up your respectability, at the expense of the feelings, and character for good sense, of those who live here and those who *have* lived here while your operations have been going forward. Though you had lost much of your attraction and popular influence, a considerable proportion of women was in your audience, especially because you were a rich man, and came from Europe. It is as common for women to be found flocking round a rich man, as butterflies round a rich slough, more especially if he has any thing of a knack at dissimulation. Whereas if you had been a poor man and born in America, and had a habit of speaking nothing but plain truth, a *hundred to ten* not two females would have been present at your meeting. Such precisely is the nature of most female education in the United States (as well as some other parts of the world) to inspire a worship of individual wealth, a reverence of every thing foreign and strange, and a contempt of what is plain. And you, sir, have done your part in practically recommending such a sort of education which inspires a veneration of wealth and a contempt of simplicity and sincerity. It seems that some how or other, your practice particularly *favours* that sort of aristocratical education, whereby mankind are inclined to set a value on wealth and personal pre-eminence, although you have borne testimony against it in your preaching.

Be assured, sir, that the people living here, and those who *have* lived here, and have retired in disgust at being disappointed altogether in the expectations you had raised by your promises to make a community, do not thank you for the statements you hold forth in this last address, inasmuch as you ascribe the cause of this default to *their characters* instead of taking the weight on your own shoulders. Hereby these people conceive themselves abusively insulted. Your aspersions are dealt out in a very specious manner; but your adroitness in shuffling on them this stigma, has not been able to elude their sensibility.

The multitude that came to this place to live, since the promulgation of your plan of this settlement, came with the expectation that property would be held in common stock, in the community, and consequently that if they should continue here, they would be obliged to make all *their* possessions common stock. They certainly came with such an impression; because they got their impression from your writings. What excitement brought them here, but that of your proclamations and doctrine? This being the case, it must be that they preferred such a state of things, to that which they abandoned. If so, it is evidently true [speaking of them generally] that they agreed and coincided in an important point of a predisposition to be members of a commonwealth; and were better prepared for a compact of that kind than any such number of persons collected together in so short a space of time, that history itself could afford an example of. Yet when they were assembled, you haughtily disregarded this obvious coincidence; and when they had put their names to a paper called a constitution, being aware of their exigence you turned to them with very polite address, and offered to sell them land and houses at an enormous price, upwards of 100 per cent. more than they cost you, and more than their market value. This was entering into the practice of the 'old system,' upon a large scale. *You*, that had preached the *new* system, went directly into the practice of the *old:* for besides this, you kept up a mercantile establishment in which was continual buying and selling for gain. You, therefore, instituted no such thing as these people expected. You made no community. You laid no foundation for one. You, however, speak very diminutively of the characters of these people; making great exceptions to your 'materials.'

After all, you say [paragraph 19th of your valedictory,] "the social system is now firmly established." What *is* this 'social system,' of which you speak? Have you ever logically defined it, unless it be inferred from your writings to be the system of commonwealths? But *here*, is no commonwealth.—Is it the social system where the property is mostly at the exclusive disposal of an individual? Where a tavern is kept, charging $3 per week for boarding, 37 1-2 cents for a meal, and 12 1-2 for a single lodging? Where a large store of merchandize is owned by an individual, retailing goods at extortionate prices much higher than those of any other trading houses in the neighboring country? Where a cotton mill is in the possession of an individual, employing poor people on scanty wages? Where the same man carries on distillation of grain into whiskey which he sells by barrels and gallons? Where you are the owner of a considerable part of the property, and lease houses and gardens to single families? Where every one shirks for himself, and gets what he can and keeps what he can get hold of, in opposition to others? Is such a state of things the social system? Then we have a social system every where; in London, in Paris, in New-York, in Vincennes, at St. Louis, and a den of thieves is a social system. No, you say, it is on the New-Harmony *lands*, and not in town. Well, now let us look into the woods surrounding New-Harmony. But here, though you have leased certain tracts to some individuals and a few families, though you have leased them cheap and for a long term, yet you are still the proprietor of the land, and it is subject to any execution that might issue against you from a court of law in this state, whether from judgment rendered upon confession or otherwise; and are those people who rent this ground and those who may join them obligated to make their property common stock and not hold any estate separate? No. Then you hold your individual property, in the real estate, and they severally hold *their* individual property. What do we find here that looks like a commonwealth? And is *here* the 'social system firmly established?' Perchance it may be found in some families of rabbits and partridges.

You proceed,—"Already eight independent communities of common property and equality, have been formed upon the New-Harmony estate, exclusive of Mr. M'Clure's or the education society, and the town of New-Harmony which has naturally become the place of reception for strangers who have a desire to join some of the existing communities or to form others."

This is all illusion. Wherein consists the independence of those infant settlements? The inhabitants are only your tenants; you bind them in certain conditions for their tenure; you are the landlord: besides, a community of common property and equality, means a state of society in which all things are common, and no member holds separate exclusive property. No such thing exists on the New-Harmony estate. So far then from eight independent communities, there is not only not *one* independent community, but there is not the foundation laid for one.

Again, paragraph 20th. " New-Harmony is therefore now literally surrounded by independent communities; and applications are made almost daily by persons who come from far and near to be permitted to establish themselves in a similar manner."

What do you imagine would be the impression one of those strangers at a distance whom you would have believe this statement, would feel upon arriving at New-Harmony after having plodded through six or seven miles of dense woods that presented no vestige of human existence, when, looking from the dome of the Hall, he could descry no trace of human culture beyond the purlieus of the village but in one direction, where the small society number 3, with a few cabins a mile east of town, presents itself, and some huts a mile beyond, where lived the community number 2, which is broken up because it could not pay its debt and interest, and which remain to be occupied by some Marylanders who are to settle under an individual to whom you have leased the land, and were told that about two miles beyond this, embosomed in the woods, is one log cottage containing four families, which constitute one of your communities, drudging like slaves to clear your ground; that besides these, a place three miles south has three or four poor families of German emigrants, just arrived in the country; and that, except one or two huts where single families live, in no other point of the compass is any inhabitant on your land? Would he not be likely to say he was mocked by your description? That he had fed upon wind? That your communities were composed of trees? But it is possible some of these will one day

visit Harmony merely for the pleasure of viewing so de-
lightsome a region as you make of it: for in the 22d paragraph, you say—

"No site for a number of communities in close union together can be
finer than that which surrounds us. Its natural situations and variety of its
productions exceed every thing of the kind I have ever seen in Europe or
America. The rich land, intermixed with islands, woods, rivers, and hills,
in a beautiful proportion to each other, presents from our high grounds a
prospect which highly gratifies every intelligent stranger."

To speak of 'land intermixed with islands,' conveys
an idea that islands are of a different nature from land.
—These islands in the *midst of the land*, or [vulgarly
speaking] *islands upon dry land*, and, as it were, *mixed in
with* the land, and woods and hills besides, must indeed
produce a surprisingly novel and romantic prospect, almost sufficiently attractive to induce some intelligent
strangers to cross the Atlantic to behold it.

"It is true, misconceptions of our proceedings and of our present state
are gone forth, to the great grief of those who were looking with intense
interest to an amelioration of the condition of all classes of society, from
the measures which were to commence here."

How could misconceptions be the source of such pain-
ful feelings in those who *had* no such misconceptions?
Certain persons were looking with deep interest to an
amelioration of the condition of all classes of society
from measures which were to commence here; and certain other persons had *misconceptions* of our proceedings
and our present state. How could these misconceptions
cause such great grief to the others? If *they* had no misconceptions themselves, how could the misconceptions
of other people give them so much trouble?—But you
have not condescended to tell us what these misconceptions are, that have gone forth. You do not point out a
single instance of a misconception, nor of a misstatement
arising out of a misconception of our proceedings or of
our present state, that any one has had or made concerning these things.—Was it a misconception that you
last October entered into a compact with about a hundred people, ·more or less, to make common stock with

them, of your estate, and they were to make common
stock of *their* estates, that you and four others of your
appointment were to govern; that this sort of government was to last five years, and that you and the other
people signed this compact? Was it a misconception
that about four months afterwards you sold out the personal property to an individual, leased him a large tract
of land, and some buildings and establishments in town,
sold the store, the tavern, and one way or other peculiarized most of the property to the control of individuals?
Was it a misconception that you sent warnings to twenty
families or more, that they must leave the place or accept of your offer of wild lands and form societies out of
town? Was it a misconception that you were continually changing your measures during the last year; that
you made a great many bargains one after another; that
you had a great many contracts, leases, bonds, indentures, orders, receipts, bills and inventories drawn?—
It is very questionable that any serious falsehood has
been told by those who left this place, concerning the
state of things here, or your proceedings.

" From the measures which were to commence here."

Certain measures *were* to commence here; but unfor-
tunately they never happened to commence: and for
this one plain reason, that you did not *permit* them to
commence, or you did not *commence* them. The measures that *were* to commence here, according to your
doctrine, and that were *expected* to commence, were,
that this estate should be held in common stock; that
the people who should inherit it should have no separate
or exclusive interest; that, having made all their private
possessions common, they should own this town in common and undivided inheritance, have equal rights and
privileges, labor according to their capacities, and be
at ease: and that those who would not act upon this
principle, should leave the place.—These are the measures which those who came here expected would com-

mence, the measures which those who did not come, but who were advocates of the social system, expected would commence, and from which they 'looked for an amelioration of the condition of all classes of society.' But these did not commence. You remained the private owner of the estate, according to the laws of peculiar property, and, holding it at your disposal, did not make it common stock. The land, the houses, the store, the goods, the money, the utensils, the cattle, were YOURS; and you did not make them common property; neither did you make it a condition of others' becoming members of the society, that *they* should make common property of all *their* private possessions. So that there was no general common stock made. It rested at your will; and you did not permit such a thing to exist as a commonwealth, or a community of common property and equality.

You are very candid, therefore, in saying '*were* to commence,' instead of saying *commenced* or *had commenced*. But you say—

" These reports have been most beneficial ; they have prevented us from being quite overwhelmed with numbers."

You make very light of the feelings of three hundred people who left this place, disappointed and in trouble, and conceiving themselves injured by you.—Here was plenty of productive land, goods, money, houses, and timber to make houses with, for the subsistence of twice as many people as all that ever quartered here. There was wanting only the will of ONE MAN, to make the appropriation as a perpetual common inheritance and the home of the abjurers of individual property and the old system of society; thence the whole mass had been set in regular easy motions, so as to subsist comfortably without any crowding. That one man was yourself.

"These operations have been going forward so successfully that perhaps no pleasure has been more pure than that which I have enjoyed for some time past in my daily visits to some one of these new establishments; where, by the industry of the persons engaged, I saw the sure foundation laid of independence for themselves and for their children's children through many generations."

What delightful sensations you must have experienced in visiting the settlement of the English farmers, which was called community No. 3, who are struggling under a debt of six or seven thousand dollars with its interest, for their land, and have to pay compound interest next year because they could not discharge the first year's interest; some of the most able bodied and industrious of whose members have gone and left them because they despaired of ever being able to pay the debt. And when you visited the cottage in the woods, with its four families, did you not observe that some were in favor of separate habitations, and others argued that they should all live and eat together as one family?

"From the new order of things arising around them, they must become a superior race of intelligent, virtuous, and happy beings, whose chief occupation after a few years of temperance and industry, will be to distribute to others the means of becoming as independent, useful, and happy as themselves."

New order of things, indeed, arising around them! eleven new log huts with glass windows (at No. 3,) of the English farmers, they having heretofore lived in rented houses in town, the people deeply in debt and likely to be in debt these twelve years, obliged to raise barley and make beer to sell for money, obliged to exert all their ingenuity to acquire wherewith to pay their taxes and interest, their debt continually increasing by compound interest;—One log hut at No. something—in the woods, with four families, and half a section of ground, under a lease with certain conditions in default of which, it is to revert, a small annual rent and the taxes to pay; eleven new log huts, with mud chimneys, and no glass, by the road side near town, the people drudging like hounds for scanty wages and taking their pay in goods at shaving prices: such is the "new order of things!"

"While preparing for my journey to Europe and just as I was going to set out, an event occurred, as you know, which arose as I must believe, from some extraordinary misconception in the minds of some of our well meaning friends, which fortunately has detained me some days longer among you."

'An event occurred.' You were very careful not to tell the public what that event was. You were cautious enough not to tell them that it was William M'Clure's prosecuting you for $40,000, to make you either reimburse his money or give him a deed in fee simple of the estate he had bought from you, that you in the mean time sent to take out a writ to prosecute him for $90,000, though in strict truth, it was supposed the balance was in his favor; that the next day [rather than you should both go to jail] you entered into arrangements, you giving him the wished-for title to the estate; and in the course of a few days closed the settlement of your books. This was the 'event' that occurred; it was only a sort of contest or squabble about individual property, between two rich men, whereof you were one. But why you should think this event arose from an 'extraordinary misconception' I do not know. It being scarcely a thing more *uncommon* for one rich man to be jealous of another rich man's cheating him and sue him for a sum of money, and for the other out of resentment or resistance to sue '*back again*' for twice as large a sum, than it is for one ram-cat to attempt to claw another ram-cat's eyes out.

This event, however, shakes the credibility of a preceding paragraph, where you say—

"I also made arrangements to settle before my departure for Europe every outstanding account against me and those concerned with me in this establishment and experiment."

Now, if you were JUST GOING TO SET OUT, and yet were liable to such an event as M'Clure's suing you for $40,000, and you had book accounts against him, and he against you, which were to settle, and which were afterwards settled, it seems as if you had not, upon the whole matter, made up your mind to settle *all* your 'affairs before you started; but were disposed to go away and leave some things unsettled.

Thus much I have thought necessary to say, for the glory of truth, concerning your last communication. Ascribe it not to personal animosity; but to my zeal for the cause of the real social system.——*Adieu.*

PAUL BROWN.

*New-Harmony, May* 25, 1827.

THE END.

# THE AMERICAN UTOPIAN ADVENTURE

sources for the study of communitarian socialism in the
United States 1680–1880

## Series One

Edward D. Andrews THE COMMUNITY INDUSTRIES OF THE
SHAKERS (1932)

Adin Ballou HISTORY OF THE HOPEDALE COMMUNITY from its
inception to its virtual submergence in the Hopedale Parish. Edited
by W. S. Heywood (1897)

Paul Brown TWELVE MONTHS IN NEW HARMONY presenting a
faithful account of the principal occurrences that have taken place
there during that period; interspersed with remarks (1827)

John S. Duss THE HARMONISTS. A personal history (1943)

Frederick W. Evans AUTOBIOGRAPHY OF A SHAKER and revelation
of the Apocalypse. With an appendix. Enlarged edition (1888)

Parke Godwin A POPULAR VIEW OF THE DOCTRINES OF CHARLES
FOURIER (1844) DEMOCRACY, CONSTRUCTIVE AND PACIFIC
(1844)

Walter C. Klein JOHANN CONRAD BEISSEL, MYSTIC AND
MARTINET, 1690–1768 (1942)

William J. McNiff HEAVEN ON EARTH: A PLANNED MORMON
SOCIETY (1940) With "Communism among the Mormons," by Hamil-
ton Gardner

Michael A. Mikkelsen THE BISHOP HILL COLONY. A religious,
communistic settlement in Henry County, Illinois (1892) With "Eric
Janson and the Bishop Hill Colony," by Silvert Erdahl

Oneida Community BIBLE COMMUNISM. A compilation from the annual
reports and other publications of the Oneida Association and its branches,
presenting, in connection with their history, a summary view of their
religious and social theories (1853)

Marianne (Dwight) Orvis LETTERS FROM BROOK FARM 1841–1847.
Edited by Amy L. Reed (1928)

Robert A. Parker A YANKEE SAINT. John Humphrey Noyes and the
Oneida Community (1935)

A. J. G. Perkins & Thersa Wolfson FRANCES WRIGHT: FREE
ENQUIRER. The study of a temperament (1939)

Jules Prudhommeaux ICARIE ET SON FONDATEUR, ÉTIENNE
CABET. Contribution à l'étude du socialisme expérimental (1907)

Albert Shaw ICARIA. A chapter in the history of communism (1884)